P9-CLX-107

Level

6

Brain-Powered
Lessons
to Engage
All Learners

Author
LaVonna Roth, M.S.Ed.

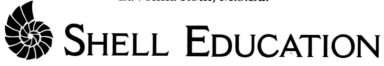

SHELL EDUCATION

Publishing Credits

Robin Erickson, *Production Director*; Lee Aucoin, *Creative Director*;
Timothy J. Bradley, *Illustration Manager*; Emily R. Smith, M.A.Ed., *Editorial Director*;
Jennifer Wilson, *Editor*; Evelyn Garcia, M.A.Ed., *Editor*; Amber Goff, *Editorial Assistant*;
Grace Alba Le, *Designer*; Corinne Burton, M.A.Ed., *Publisher*

Image Credits

All images Shutterstock
DRCD Images from Library of Congress: [LC-USF33- 006034-M2], [HABS ID,8-PLAVI.V,2--2], [LC-USF33- 000110-M1]

Standards

© 2004 Mid-continent Research for Education and Learning (McREL)
© 2007 Teachers of English to Speakers of Other Languages, Inc. (TESOL)
© 2007 Board of Regents of the University of Wisconsin System. World-Class Instructional Design and Assessment (WIDA)
© 2010 National Governors Association Center for Best Practices and Council of Chief State School Officers (CCSS)

Shell Education

5301 Oceanus Drive
Huntington Beach, CA 92649-1030
http://www.shelleducation.com
ISBN 978-1-4258-1183-9
© 2014 Shell Educational Publishing, Inc.

Table of Contents

Introduction

A Letter to You 5

About the Author 6

The Power of the Brain 7

Strategy Overviews 12

How to Use This Book 20

Correlation to the Standards 24

Standards Chart 25

Content Area Correlations Chart 28

Kinesthetic Word Web Lessons

M.A.I.N. Causes of World War I 29

Express Yourself 34

Water and Weather 40

Thinking About Themes 46

It Takes Two Lessons

Themes Across Genres 51

Depression and Recession: Same or Different? 55

Perspectives on Anne Frank 59

Show It with Dough! Lessons

Roots of the Civil War 62

Solar System Sculptures 64

Fascinating Figures (of Speech) 67

I'm in the Pic Lessons

Precise Prose 69

Variability in Pictures 78

Fascinating Fossils 83

Table of Contents

Response Cards Lessons

Making a Claim 88

Lines and Planes: Mapping Rational Numbers 93

Word Detective 99

Matchmaker Lessons

Revolutionary War Leaders 105

Equivalent Expressions 109

Investigating Inferences 116

Just Say It Lessons

Perfect Paragraphs 121

Rad Ratios 126

Energy: A Case of Multiple Identities 135

Reverse, Reverse! Lessons

Women and War 140

Equivalent Numbers: One Quantity, Many Forms 144

Inquiry and Investigation 153

Appendices

Appendix A: References Cited 158

Appendix B: Contents of the Digital Resource CD 160

Judy,
To my International touring buddy! It was such a pleasure to meet you in Beirut, Lebanon next time I can't wait to see another museum... mosque... torrential downpour or center of a city. Thank you for all you do for educators. You rock! and to continue our tours.
Your friend,
LaVonne

A Letter to You

Dear Educator,

I want to take a moment to thank you for the inspiration that you are! As more mandates fall upon your shoulders and changes are made, I admire your drive, passion, and willingness to keep putting our students first. Every decision we make as educators should come down to one simple question: "Is this decision in the best interest of our students?" This reflects not our opinion, our philosophy, or our own agenda, but simply what is going to make the greatest impact on our students in preparing them for life and career.

As you continue to be the best you can be, I want you to take a few moments each day, look in the mirror, and smile. Come on—I know you can give me a bigger smile than that! Go for the big Cheshire Cat smile with all teeth showing. Why? Because you are sometimes your greatest cheerleader. Now, take that same smile and pass it on to colleagues, students, and parents. Attitude is catching—so let's share the one that puts smiles on others' faces! You will feel better and your day will be better.

Now, tear out this page. Tape it to a place where you will see it every... single... day. Yep! Tear it out. Tape it to the bathroom mirror, your dashboard, your desk—wherever you are sure to see it. Recite and do the following every single day—no joke.

I am appreciated!

I am amazing!

I am the difference!

From one educator to another, thank you for all you do!

—LaVonna Roth

P.S. Be sure to connect with me on social media! I would love to hear from you on these strategies and lessons.

About the Author

LaVonna Roth, M.S.Ed., is an international author, speaker, and consultant. She has had the privilege of working with teachers on three continents, sharing her passion for education and how the brain learns. Her desire to keep the passion of engaging instructional delivery is evident in her ideas, presentations, workshops, and books.

LaVonna has the unique ability to teach some of the more challenging concepts in education and make them simple and doable. Her goal is for teachers to be reenergized, to experience ideas that are practical and applicable, and have a great impact on student achievement because of the effect these strategies have on how the brain learns.

As a full-time teacher, LaVonna taught students at the elementary and secondary levels in all content areas, students in ELL and gifted programs, and those in the regular classroom. Her educational degrees include a bachelor's degree in special education—teaching the hearing impaired—and two master's degrees, one in the art of teaching and another in educational leadership. In addition to other professional organizations, LaVonna serves as a board member for Florida ASCD and is an affiliate member of the Society for Neuroscience.

As an author, she has written a powerful resource notebook, *Brain-Powered Strategies to Engage All Learners*, and is a dynamic and engaging presenter.

When LaVonna isn't traveling and speaking, she relaxes by spending time with her family in the Tampa, Florida area. She is dedicated to putting students first and supporting teachers to be the best they can be.

Acknowledgements

My family
My friends
All educators
Teacher Created Materials staff

I believe we accomplish great things when we surround ourselves with great people and take action. Thank you for all you do!

—LaVonna Roth

The Power of the Brain

"What actually changes in the brain are the strengths of the connections of neurons that are engaged together, moment by moment, in time."

—Dr. Michael Merzenich

The brain is a very powerful organ, one we do not completely understand or know everything about. Yet science reveals more and more to us each day.

As educators, we have a duty to understand how the brain learns so that we can best teach our students. If we do not have an understanding of some of the powerful tools that can help facilitate our teaching and allow us to better target the brain and learning, we lose a lot of time with our students that could be used to serve them better. Plus, the likelihood of doing as much reteaching will lessen.

This is where *Brain-Powered Lessons to Engage All Learners* comes in! The eight strategies included within the lessons are designed around how the brain learns as a foundation. In addition, they are meant to be used as a formative assessment, include higher-order thinking, increase the level of engagement in learning, and support differentiation. For detailed information on each strategy, see pages 12–19.

What Makes the Brain Learn Best

As you explore the strategies in this book, keep the following key ideas in mind.

The content being taught and learned must:

◎ be engaging

◎ be relevant

◎ make sense

◎ make meaning

◎ involve movement

◎ support memory retention

The Power of the Brain *(cont.)*

Be Engaging

In order for students to pay attention, we must engage the brain. This is the overarching theme to the rest of the elements. Too often, students are learning complacently. Just because students are staring at the teacher, with pencil in hand and taking notes, does not mean they are engaged. For example, we know that they are engaged when they answer questions or are interacting with the information independently with a teacher or another student. We don't always know when they are engaged just by looking at them. Sometimes, it's a simple question or observation of what they are doing that helps identify this. Body language can tell us a lot, but do not rely on this as the only point of observation. Many teachers may have not gone into teaching to "entertain," but entertaining is one component of being engaging. As neuroscience research has revealed, it was noted as early as 1762 that the brain does change (neuroplasticity) based on experiences (Doidge 2007). It rewires itself based upon experiences and new situations, creating new neural pathways. "Even simple brain exercises such as presenting oneself with challenging intellectual environments, interacting in social situations, or getting involved in physical activities will boost the general growth of connections" (HOPES 2010, §2). This is fantastic if we are creating an environment and lessons that are positive and planned in a way that fires more neurons that increase accurate learning.

> **"Even simple brain exercises such as presenting oneself with challenging intellectual environments, interacting in social situations, or getting involved in physical activities will boost the general growth of connections"** (HOPES 2010, §2).

The Power of the Brain *(cont.)*

As a reflection for you, think about the following with respect to student engagement:

◎ What are the students doing during the lesson? Are they doing something with the information that shows they are into it? Are they asking questions? Are they answering?

◎ What is their body language showing? Are they slumped, or are they sitting in a more alert position? Are their eyes glazed and half-closed, or are they bright, alert, and paying attention to where their focus should be?

◎ Who is doing most of the talking and thinking? Move away from being the sage on the stage! Let the students be the stars. Share your knowledge with them in increments, but permit them to interact or explore.

◎ What could you turn over to students to have them create a way to remember the content or ask questions they have? What could be done to change up the lessons so they are interacting or standing? Yes, parts of lessons can be taught by having students stand for a minute or so. Before they sit, have them stretch or high-five a few classmates to break up the monotony.

Be Relevant

Why should the brain want to learn and remember something that has no relevance to us? If we want our students to learn information, it is important that we do what we can to make the information relevant. An easy way to achieve this is by bringing in some background knowledge that students have about the topic or making a personal connection. This does not need to take long.

As you will note, the lessons in this book start out with modeling. Modeling allows learners to have an understanding of the strategy and it also takes a moment to bring in what they know and, when possible, to make a personal connection. Consider asking students what they know about a topic and have them offer ideas. Or ask them to reflect on a piece of literature that you read or to ponder a question you have provided. For English language learners, this strategy is particularly effective when they can relate it to something of which they have a foundational concept and can make a connection to what they are learning. The language will come.

Make Sense

Is what you are teaching something that makes sense to students? Do they see the bigger picture or context? If students are making sense of what they are learning, a greater chance of it moving from working memory to long-term memory will increase. Some students can be asked if the idea makes sense and if they clearly understand. If they are able to explain it in their own words, they probably have a good grasp on metacognition and where they are in their learning. Other students may need to be coached to retell you what they just learned.

The Power of the Brain *(cont.)*

Make Meaning

Once students have had an opportunity to make sense of what they are learning, provide an opportunity for them to make meaning. This means that they have a chance to apply what was learned and actually "play" with the skills or concepts. Are they able to complete some tasks or provide questions on their own? Are they ready to take the information to higher levels that demonstrate the depth of understanding? (Refer to Webb's Depth of Knowledge for some additional insight into various levels of making meaning on pages 22–23.) For some students, simply asking a few questions related to what is being taught or having them write a reflection of what was just explained will allow you to check in on their understanding to see where they are before taking their thinking to a higher or a deeper level.

Involve Movement

This one is particularly important because of the plethora of research on movement. Dr. John Ratey wrote the book *Spark*, which documents how student achievement soars based on some changes made to students' physical education program in which students achieved their target heart-rate zone during their physical education time. Movement, particularly exercise, increases brain-derived neurotrophic factors (BDNF) that increase learning and memory (Vaynman, Ying, and Gomez-Pinilla 2004).

Knowing that getting students to achieve their target heart rate zone is not always an option, do what you can. Have students take some brain breaks that heighten their heart rate—even if for just a minute.

Movement has strong retention implications in other ways. Students can create a gesture connected to the lesson concept, or they can stand and move while they make meaning from what they learned. Movement is multisensory, thus, various regions of the brain are activated. When multiple brain pathways are stimulated, they are more likely to enter long-term potentiation from activating episodic and semantic memories.

If you come across a model lesson in this book in which not much movement is shared, or you find your students have been sitting longer than you may wish (you will know because their body language will tell you—unfortunately, we should have had them moving before this point), my challenge to you is to think of what movement you can add to the lesson. It could involve a gesture, a manipulative, or physically getting up and moving. If you are concerned about them calming back down, set your expectations and stick to them. Keep in mind that often when students "go crazy" when permitted to move, it's probably because they *finally* get to move. Try simple techniques to bring students back into focus. "Part of the process of assisting children in developing necessary skills is getting to the root of why they behave as they do" (Harris and Goldberg 2012, xiv).

The Power of the Brain *(cont.)*

Support Memory Retention

If we want our students to retain what we teach them, then it is important that we keep in mind what causes our brains to retain that information.

Key Elements to Memory Retention	Why
Emotions	We can create an episodic memory when we connect emotions to our learning.
Repetition	Repetition increases memory as long as there is engagement involved. Worksheets and drill and kill do not serve long-term memory well.
Patterns/Organization	When our brains take in messages, they begin to file the information by organizing it into categories.
Personal connection	Linking learning to one's self is a powerful brain tool for memory. This, too, can be tied to emotion, making an even stronger connection.
Linking new and prior knowledge	Taking in new information automatically results in connecting past knowledge to what is new.

(Roth 2012)

As you explore the strategies and lessons throughout this book, note how many of them incorporate the keys to memory retention and what engages our students' brains. As you begin to explore the use of these strategies on your own, be sure to keep the framework of those important components.

The bottom line—explore, have fun, and ask your students how they feel about lessons taught. They will tell you if they found the lesson interesting, engaging, and relevant. So get in there, dig in, and have some fun with your students while trying out these strategies and lessons!

Kinesthetic Word Webs
Strategy Overview

Movement is crucial to learning. We must move because the "sit-and-get" method is overused and not as effective as when we have the chance to increase our oxygen intake and shift the activity. Although there is no exact science as to the number of minutes that elapse before we should move or change direction, no more than 20 minutes is an adequate amount of time for learning to occur before we do something with what was learned (Schenck 2005). Our working memory can only hold so much information before it becomes fatigued or bored (Sousa 2006). Thus, implementing the suggested 20-minute time frame into teaching should help teachers to remember the importance of chunking material and allowing time for the brain to process material being learned.

We know what a web is on paper, but what is a Kinesthetic Word Web? It is a strategy that gets students up and moving with the content of the lessons. Picture a word web on paper. Now, turn the outer ovals on the word web into students and imagine their arms touching the person's shoulder in the center oval. That is a *Kinesthetic Word Web*.

Strategy Insight

The *Kinesthetic Word Webs* strategy is designed to take a paper-and-pencil activity and add movement and challenge to raise the level of engagement. As Wolfe and Brandt (1998) stated, "The brain likes a challenge!" It seeks patterns. Patterns are required during this strategy in order to be successful.

Teacher Notes

◎ Be sure every student has a card. Do not worry about every student fitting into a word web. If a student cannot be a part of a Kinesthetic Word Web because his or her word has already appeared in the web or because there was not an exact number of students for each set, they can explain where they would go and why.

◎ **Note:** Some students do not like to be touched, so knowing students and their backgrounds is very important. As an alternative, they can each place a fist on a hip and connect elbow to elbow; they can extend a leg and touch foot to foot; or you can provide 15 inches of string to each student, with the center student holding one end of all the strings.

It Takes Two
Strategy Overview

In this strategy, students compare and contrast two topics (e.g., stories, historical figures, types of clouds and shapes) using a T-chart and sticky notes. The goal is for students to analyze each topic and create a chart that represents their thinking. Thereafter, another group of students will evaluate whether it agrees with the original group's thoughts or, if not, if it is going to propose another way to think about the topic. The goal is for students to be able to think at a higher level by justifying either what each sticky note says and where each one is placed or if it qualifies to be on the T-chart at all.

Strategy Insight

Organization and thinking critically are key components in this strategy. Since we organize ideas in our brains systematically and create a neural pathway as more modalities are used, students increase their learning by seeing the information, sorting through what is important, organizing the facts by what is similar and what is different, and adding another level of value through student interaction (Van Tassell 2004). Each of these components plays an integral part in student engagement and retention (Covington 2000). It is another way for students to work with content at a level that is minds-on and hands-on.

Using sticky notes during this activity is important (as opposed to recording the similarities and differences on a sheet) because students' thinking will shift as they discuss and learn more. The sticky notes allow the graphic organizer to become manipulative, and it is a new way for them to see if they agree or disagree with their classmates and adjust accordingly.

Teacher Notes

◎ It is imperative that teachers observe during all stages of the lesson. This provides the feedback we need to determine the next direction of instruction. In addition, it allows an opportunity to guide students in their thinking, as some may struggle with concepts at a higher level. **Note:** Do not guide too much. A large part of learning is struggling through the process with a small amount of frustration but not so much that students give up.

◎ During discussions, students will likely discover that there can be more than one answer. That is where collaboration and cooperation pay off.

◎ For younger students, reconvene as a whole group and model the evaluation steps, using one group's chart.

Show It with Dough!
Strategy Overview

Our brains recall pictures quite well. This phenomenon is called the *Pictorial Superiority Effect* (PSE) (Medina 2008). Simply put, the brain grasps pictures and can recognize and recall a picture with far less effort than it takes to recall text.

Through the use of dough sculptures, students think about a concept and make a three-dimensional representation, often moving from abstract to concrete ideas. This is a higher-level skill since it requires extended thinking to represent something in a new way (Bloom 1956).

Strategy Insight

Many concepts we teach are quite abstract, particularly as students progress in grade levels. This strategy often requires students to visualize the concept on a concrete level rather than an abstract level. Thus, this strategy is at a higher level because students are being asked to demonstrate their learning in a new way. Additionally, we are asking students to connect their visual representations to what they already know; therefore, we also incorporate activating prior knowledge and experiences, which in turn ties in to something personal. This strategy can also impact other content areas and allows students the opportunity to use their creativity in an expressive way.

Teacher Notes

◎ Walk around as students create their sculptures and ask them to think about what they are making and why. Consider doing this very quietly so others do not hear what they are creating, or use written communication.

◎ Place student sculptures on cardboard so they are easy to move or display.

◎ After students add more detail to their sculptures and write their stories, display them where others can enjoy them.

I'm in the Pic
Strategy Overview

I'm in the Pic is a strategy that targets various modalities for storage of memory in the brain. The more students can experience this strategy the better, because each of our senses is stored in different regions of the brain (Medina 2008). The way we learn the information dictates where much of the memory is stored and connected.

We can compare using our senses and experiences to when you learned how to ride a bike. Try to recall the approximate time of day and location of that first bike-riding experience. This is called *episodic memory*, as it refers to an event (or an episode) in your life (Sousa 2006; Sprenger 1999). Your episodic memory deals with time and location. Now, let us add emotion to this memory. As you learned to ride, you experienced movement and wind blowing in your face.

However, providing actual sensory experiences for all content is not always possible. So try engaging students' senses through a *relational memory*. According to Willis (2008), relational memory is the process of connecting new experiences to something we already have in our stored memory. For example, you can connect the feeling of the wind in your face while riding in a car with the windows down to the feeling of the wind blowing in your face while riding a bike.

[handwritten note: memory Encodeg ↓ willis]

[handwritten note: Top Down Atten]

Strategy Insight

Students are shown a picture and then asked to imagine that they are in the picture. They are asked to describe what they see. When teachers are working with students on this skill, they should keep asking, "What else do you see?" This reminds students to pay attention to detail. Since paying attention is a skill that has to be taught, teachers can work with students by giving them practice that is engaging, particularly if they choose pictures that are colorful, unusual, close up, or intriguing (Jensen 2006). The right brain creates the gist, or context of experiences, and the overall meaning of events (Siegel 2001). As students pay attention to the details, the teacher should be prepared to be amazed at what students can pick out! The teacher can continue the strategy by asking students to consider what they might touch, hear, smell, or taste. If students say, "I think it would sound loud" when looking at a picture of a busy city with cars bumper-to-bumper, then the teacher can ask, "What do you see that supports your thinking?" It is beneficial for students to do the thinking and articulate the reasoning behind their thinking. The goal is to increase engagement, improve their attention to detail, tap in to the emotions of what it would be like to be in the picture, and use multiple senses to help remember.

[handwritten note: Top Down Atten att to detail]

[handwritten note: multisen]

Teacher Notes

◎ At the start of the lesson, use a picture that is engaging and one that students have experience with as you walk through the process.

◎ Understand that modeling is required for students to learn how to identify background knowledge, relate it to what they know, or imagine the experience of what it would be like to be "in" the picture.

Response Cards
Strategy Overview

This strategy allows the teacher to receive a response from each student within a short time frame, and it provides the feedback you need to drive instruction. Once students have responded, they discuss their thinking with a partner. This is the teacher's opportunity to listen in on their conversations. If they got the answer right, was it for the right reason? If it was wrong, where did their thinking go astray?

Post higher-order thinking question stems around the room. Teach students how to use these stems to ask questions. If teachers want to raise the level of inquiry and understanding, students need the resources to do so, which include modeling how to ask a question that taps into thinking and then allowing them to question (Hunter 1993). By doing this, students become more metacognitively aware by figuring out the connections they made (Baker 2009). What did they know beforehand that helped them connect the question asked to their response? If they were struggling between two answers, what were they thinking that caused them to choose one answer? Another great technique to encourage depth of thinking is to ask open-ended questions, such as *Why?* or *How do you know?* (Sprenger 1999; Willis 2006). When students provide an answer followed up by *why* or *how do you know*, their initial reaction may be that they are wrong, which sends them into a thinking mode to figure out where they went wrong. Share with students that they may not be wrong; encourage them to think their answers through.

Strategy Insight

Response Cards are an alternate way to formatively assess students' thinking without using whiteboards. Since our brain's attention piques with novelty, Response Cards allow students to give teachers feedback in a different way. Students think independently, respond, and then show their answers. Students receive premade Response Cards that have answers on them, or older students can write the answers themselves. Answers on the Response Cards should be written in the same location so they can quickly be seen and checked for accuracy.

When students share their answers, it is important they justify their thinking. This allows them to make connections and take the strategy to a higher level. The teacher should listen to students as they talk with others to see if their thinking is correct. This gives the teacher an insight into students' thinking. Plus, knowing they hold them accountable helps with classroom management.

Teacher Notes

◎ When students share their thinking with partners, it is important to listen in to see if there are any misconceptions or to find out who is struggling with the concept.

◎ Encourage students to know it is acceptable to question authority in a respectful manner. Just because something is said by an authority figure does not mean it is always right.

Matchmaker
Strategy Overview

The importance of movement and having students get up out of their seats cannot be emphasized enough. Thus, here is another strategy that allows our students to do so. *Matchmaker* also provides students an opportunity to get repeated practice in an environment in which the repetition is guided and correct. This means that when students practice repeatedly, the likelihood of recall increases. A key factor here is that it must be correct practice. When students do this activity with one another, they are getting a chance to see repeated practice with automatic feedback provided about whether they are correct or not.

Strategy Insight

Every student is given an address label to wear. Each label is a vocabulary word, a concept, a formula, etc. On index cards are the matching definitions, illustrations, examples, synonyms, etc.

Students wear the address label and stand in a circle with the index cards on the floor in the middle. Students hold hands and bend down to pick up an index card with their connected hands. Without letting go, they have to get the card they picked up to the correct person, according to his or her address label. This strategy can be repeated as many times as you wish to help students practice.

Teacher Notes

◎ An alternative to this is for students to not hold hands when they pick up a card. However, energy and engagement increase with the added challenge of holding hands and not letting go.

◎ Be sure to listen in and encourage students to discuss disagreements or to have them respond to a reason why a particular card goes with another card.

Just Say It
Strategy Overview

Working together and hearing thoughts and language are beneficial to all learners, but can be especially beneficial to English language learners. *Just Say It* permits students to not only use what they have read, written, or heard but have a chance to use listening skills for the content as well. A challenge layer to this strategy is having students hold back on a response for a period of time. This allows the other student to say what he or she needs to say before the other student inflicts his or her opinion or factual information upon them. It teaches the skill of patience, listening, and being open to others' thoughts at the same time.

Strategy Insight

Students are to respond to their partners, providing feedback and information on a given topic (e.g., a writing prompt, thoughts, an idea). Have students sit facing their partners (sitting at desks is preferable). Identify Partner *A* as the person closest to the front of the room and Partner *B* as the person closest to the back of room. Have Partner *A* start. Partner *A* shares his or her thinking with Partner *B* as Partner *B* only listens for 30 seconds. After 30 seconds, Partner *B* responds to Partner *A*. They then switch roles—Partner *B* shares while *A* listens. Then *A* provides insight or feedback. Students should record (during or at the end) what their partners say for further consideration, and use that to write about the topic.

Teacher Notes

◎ You may wish to shorten or lengthen the time each partner has, depending upon the topic and age.

◎ Using a timer, a train whistle, or a bell is a great way to help partners know when to switch, since conversations may get lively or partners may tune out other nearby sounds.

Reverse, Reverse!
Strategy Overview

Reverse, Reverse! is meant to be a challenging strategy. When students are under stress, there will often be not only a chemical but a physical change in the brain. Students must learn the skills to deal with stress, but in a safe and friendly environment. In this strategy, students will practice the speed and fluency of facts, but they will do so under pressure—a pressure that you can adjust or increase, depending upon the topic and age level of your students.

Strategy Insight

Students sit or stand in a circle. They are given a topic and asked to brainstorm what they know about it. One student begins by sharing a fact about the topic. Going clockwise, the next student must quickly say another fact related to the one just stated. If the student pauses more than five seconds or states an incorrect fact, the student that just finished must state the next fact (reversing the direction of participation). One student sits out to judge the facts and make sure rules are followed. Continue until participation stalls. For example, a math activity using this strategy can include counting by threes. The first student says, "3;" the next student says, "6;" the next says, "9." If the following student says, "13," the rotation reverses to the previous student, who must say, "Reverse," and must also say the correct answer, "12." The responses are now going counterclockwise. An example of using this strategy in social studies can include the three branches of government. The first student might say, "Legislative branch;" the second says, "Makes the laws;" the third student says, "Congress;" and the fourth says, "Checks and balances." The judge (student sitting out) can halt the flow to ask how the response relates to a previously said fact. If justified, the round continues. *Reverse, Reverse!* continues until a predetermined amount of clock time or number of times around the circle has been met.

Teacher Notes

◎ It is important to set the stage for students to feel safe when using this strategy. You may wish to take out the reverse portion at first and work on just the speed. Add the extra layer of difficulty for novelty and time-pressured practice.

◎ For younger students, you may choose to not have the next student say, "Reverse," but instead state the correct fact.

How to Use This Book

Lesson Overview

The following lesson components are in each lesson and establish the flow and success of the lessons.

Icons state the brain-powered strategy and one of the four content areas addressed in the book: language arts, mathematics, science, or social studies.

Each lesson revolves around one of the eight **brain-powered strategies** in this book. Be sure to review the description of each strategy found on pages 12–19.

Vocabulary that will be addressed in the lesson is called out in case extra support is needed.

The **procedures** provide step-by-step instructions on how to implement the lessons successfully.

The **standard** indicates the objective for the lesson.

A **materials** list identifies the components of the lesson.

Many lessons contain a **preparation note** that indicates action needed prior to implementing the lessons. Be sure to review these notes to ensure a successful delivery of the lesson.

The **model** section of the lesson provides teachers the opportunity to model what is expected of students and what needs to be accomplished throughout the lesson.

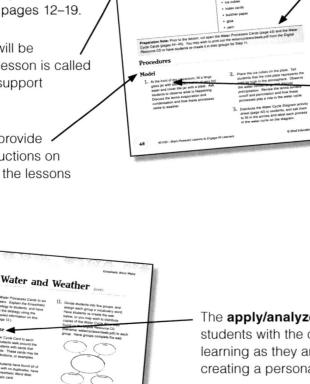

The **apply/analyze** section of the lesson provides students with the opportunity to apply what they are learning as they analyze the content and work toward creating a personal connection.

The **evaluate/create** section of the lesson provides students with the opportunity to think critically about the work of others and then to take ownership of their learning by designing the content in a way that makes sense to them.

How to Use This Book (cont.)

Lesson Overview (cont.)

Some lessons require **activity cards** to be used. You may wish to laminate the activity cards for added durability. Be sure to read the preparation note in each lesson to prepare the activity cards, when applicable.

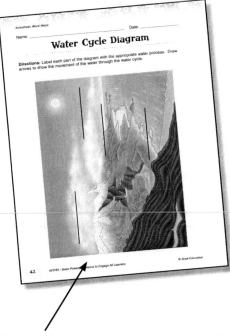

Activity sheets are included for lessons that require them. They are to be used either in groups, individually, or just by the teacher. If students are working in groups, encourage them to create a group name to label the activity sheet.

All of the activity sheets and additional teacher resources can be found on the **Digital Resource CD**.

How to Use This Book (cont.)

Implementing Higher-Order Thinking in the Lessons

What Is Higher-Order Thinking?

Higher-order thinking occurs on a different level than memorizing facts or telling something back to someone exactly the way it was told (Thomas and Thorne 2009). As educators, it is important to be aware of the level of thinking that students are asked to do. If teachers record the number of questions they ask students on a recall or restate level as well as how many were asked at a higher level, they may be surprised at the imbalance. How do they expect students to think at a higher level if they are not challenged with higher-order questions and problems? Students should be given questions and assignments that require higher-order thinking.

Higher-order thinking also involves critical thinking. If teachers want students to remember facts and think critically, they need to have them be engaged and working with the content at a higher level so that it creates understanding and depth. In addition, higher-order thinking and critical thinking are imperative to 21st century skills. Employers want workers who can problem-solve and work cooperatively to find multiple solutions. The lessons in this resource gradually place more ownership of the learning process in the hands of students as they simultaneously move through higher-order thinking.

Bloom's Taxonomy and Webb's Depth of Knowledge

Throughout the history of education, structures were created to guide teachers in ways to evoke higher-order thinking. Two of the more popular structures are Bloom's Taxonomy and Webb's Depth of Knowledge (DOK).

Benjamin Bloom developed Bloom's Taxonomy as a way to classify educational learning objectives in a hierarchy. In 2001, Lorin Anderson, a former student of Bloom's, worked with some teachers to revise Bloom's original taxonomy by changing the terminology into verbs and switching the top two levels so that *create* (synthesis) is at the top and *evaluate* (evaluation) is just below (Overbaugh and Schultz n.d.).

Norman Webb created Depth of Knowledge in 1997 in order to assist with aligning the depth and complexity of a standard with its assessment. This structure focuses on how the verb is used in the context of what is asked of the student (Webb 2005). DOK correlates with Backwards Planning (Wiggins and McTighe 2005) in that the standards are addressed first and then an assessment that targets the standards is developed or selected.

How to Use This Book *(cont.)*

It is important that teachers instruct students at cognitive levels that meet their needs while challenging them as well. Whether students are below level, on level, or above level, teachers should use the tools necessary to help them succeed. Using Webb's DOK gives us the tools to look at the end result and tie complexity to the assessment. Bloom's Taxonomy helps to guide depth of assignments and questions. Where the two meet is with the word complexity. Complexity is rigor. Complexity is the changing of levels within Bloom's, and DOK is the amount of depth of thinking that must occur. We want rigor, and thus we want complexity in our teachings.

Bloom's Taxonomy	Webb's Depth of Knowledge
Knowledge/Remembering The recall of specifics and universals, involving little more than bringing to mind the appropriate material.	**Recall** The recall of a fact, information, or procedure (e.g., What are three critical-skill cues for the overhand throw?).
Comprehension/Understanding The ability to process knowledge on a low level such that the knowledge can be reproduced or communicated without a verbatim repetition.	**Skill/Concept** The use of information, conceptual knowledge, procedures, two or more steps, etc.
Application/Applying The ability to use information in another familiar situation.	**Strategy Thinking** Requires reasoning, developing a plan or sequence of steps; has some complexity; more than one possible answer.
Analysis/Analyzing The ability to break information into parts to explore understandings and relationships.	**Extended Thinking** Requires an investigation as well as time to think and process multiple conditions of the problem or task.
Synthesis and Evaluation/Evaluating and Creating Putting together elements and parts to form a whole and then making value judgements about the method.	

Adapted from Wyoming School Health and Physical Education (2001)

Correlation to the Standards

Shell Education is committed to producing educational materials that are research and standards based. In this effort, we have correlated all of our products to the academic standards of all 50 states, the District of Columbia, the Department of Defense Dependents Schools, and all Canadian provinces.

How to Find Standards Correlations

To print a customized correlation report of this product for your state, visit our website at http://www.shelleducation.com and follow the on-screen directions. If you require assistance in printing correlation reports, please contact our Customer Service department at 1-877-777-3450.

Purpose and Intent of Standards

Legislation mandates that all states adopt academic standards that identify the skills students will learn in kindergarten through grade twelve. Many states also have standards for Pre–K. This same legislation sets requirements to ensure the standards are detailed and comprehensive.

Standards are designed to focus instruction and guide adoption of curricula. Standards are statements that describe the criteria necessary for students to meet specific academic goals. They define the knowledge, skills, and content students should acquire at each level. Standards are also used to develop standardized tests to evaluate students' academic progress. Teachers are required to demonstrate how their lessons meet state standards. State standards are used in the development of all of our products, so educators can be assured they meet the academic requirements of each state.

Common Core State Standards

Many lessons in this book are aligned to the Common Core State Standards (CCSS). The standards support the objectives presented throughout the lessons and are provided on the Digital Resource CD (filename: standards.pdf).

TESOL and WIDA Standards

The lessons in this book promote English language development for English language learners. The standards listed on the Digital Resource CD (filename: standards.pdf) support the language objectives presented throughout the lessons.

Standards Chart

Common Core State Standard	Lesson(s)
Language.6.4.b—Use common, grade-appropriate Greek or Latin affixes and roots as clues to the meaning of a word	Word Detective p. 99
Reading: Informational Text.6.9—Compare and contrast one author's presentation of events with that of another (e.g., a memoir written by someone and a biography of the same person)	Perspectives on Anne Frank p. 59
Reading: Literature.6.1—Cite textual evidence to support analysis of what the text says explicitly as well as inferences drawn from the text	Investigating Inferences p. 116
Reading: Literature.6.2—Determine a theme or a central idea of a text and how it is conveyed through particular details; provide a summary of the text distinct from personal opinions or judgments	Thinking About Themes p. 46
Reading: Literature.6.4—Determine the meaning of words and phrases as they are used in a text, including figurative and connotative meanings; analyze the impact of a specific word choice on meaning and tone	Fascinating Figures (of Speech) p. 67
Reading: Literature.6.9.a—Apply grade 6 Reading standards to literature (e.g., "Compare and contrast texts in different forms or genres [e.g., stories and poems; historical novels and fantasy stories] in terms of their approaches to similar themes and topics")	Themes Across Genres p. 51
Writing.6.1—Write arguments to support claims with clear reasons and relevant evidence	Making a Claim p. 88
Writing.6.2.b—Develop the topic with relevant facts, definitions, concrete details, quotations, or other information and examples	Perfect Paragraphs p. 121
Writing.6.2.d—Use precise language and domain-specific vocabulary to inform about or explain the topic	Precise Prose p. 69
Math 6.EE.2.b—Identify parts of an expression using mathematical terms (sum, term, product, factor, quotient, coefficient); view one or more parts of an expression as a single entity. For example, describe the expression 2 (8 + 7) as a product of two factors; view (8 + 7) as both a single entity and a sum of two terms	Express Yourself p. 34

Standards Chart *(cont.)*

Common Core State Standard	Lesson(s)
Math 6.EE.3—Apply the properties of operations to generate equivalent expressions. For example, apply the distributive property to the expression 3 (2 + x) to produce the equivalent expression 6 + 3x; apply the distributive property to the expression 24x + 18y to produce the equivalent expression 6 (4x + 3y); apply properties of operations to y + y + y to produce the equivalent expression 3y	Equivalent Expressions p. 109
Math 6.NS.6.c—Find and position integers and other rational numbers on a horizontal or a vertical number line diagram; find and position pairs of integers and other rational numbers on a coordinate plane	Lines and Planes: Mapping Rational Numbers p. 93
Math 6.RP.1—Understand the concept of a ratio, and use ratio language to describe a ratio relationship between two quantities. For example, "The ratio of wings to beaks in the bird house at the zoo was 2:1, because for every 2 wings, there was 1 beak." "For every vote candidate A received, candidate C received nearly 3 votes"	Rad Ratios p. 126
Math 6.SP.1—Recognize a statistical question as one that anticipates variability in the data related to the question and accounts for it in the answers. For example, "How old am I?" is not a statistical question, but "How old are the students in my school?" is a statistical question because one anticipates variability in students' ages	Variability in Pictures p. 78

McREL Standard	Lesson(s)
Math 2.1—Understands the relationships among equivalent number representations (e.g., whole numbers, positive and negative integers, fractions, ratios, decimals, percents, scientific notation, exponentials) and the advantages and disadvantages of each type of representation	Equivalent Numbers: One Quantity, Many Forms p. 144
Science 1.2—Knows the processes involved in the water cycle (e.g., evaporation, condensation, precipitation, surface runoff, percolation) and their effects on climatic patterns	Water and Weather p. 40

Standards Chart *(cont.)*

McREL Standard	Lesson(s)
Science 3.1—Knows characteristics and movement patterns of the planets in our Solar System	Solar System Sculptures p. 64
Science 7.2—Knows that the fossil record, through geologic evidence, documents the appearance, diversification, and extinction of many life forms	Fascinating Fossils p. 83
Science 9.1—Knows that energy is a property of many substances (e.g., heat energy is in the disorderly motion of molecules and in radiation; chemical energy is in the arrangement of atoms; mechanical energy is in moving bodies or in elastically distorted shapes; electrical energy is in the attraction or repulsion between charges)	Energy: A Case of Multiple Identities p. 135
Science 12.3—Designs and conducts a scientific investigation (e.g., formulates hypotheses, designs and executes investigations, interprets data, synthesizes evidence into explanations)	Inquiry and Investigation p. 153
Social Studies 6.4—Understands the major developments and chronology of the Revolutionary War and the roles of its political, military, and diplomatic leaders (e.g., George Washington, Benjamin Franklin, Thomas Jefferson, John Adams, Samuel Adams, John Hancock, Richard Henry Lee)	Revolutionary War Leaders p. 105
Social Studies 13—Understands the causes of the Civil War	Roots of the Civil War p. 62
Social Studies 23—Understands the causes of the Great Depression and how it affected American society	Depression and Recession: Same or Different? p. 55
Social Studies 29.3—Understands the development of the post-World War II women's movement (e.g., the major issues affecting women and the conflicts these issues engendered, the emergence of the National Organization for Women, post-World War II attitudes toward women)	Women and War p. 140
Social Studies 39.1—Understands the origins and significant features of World War I (e.g., the precipitating causes of the war; the factors that led to military stalemate in some areas; which countries joined each of the two alliances—the Allied Powers and the Central Powers—and the advantages and disadvantages for the formation of alliances; major areas of combat in Europe and Southwest Asia)	M.A.I.N. Causes of World War I p. 29

Standards Chart *(cont.)*

TESOL and WIDA Standard	Lesson(s)
English language learners **communicate** for **social**, **intercultural**, and **instructional** purposes within the school setting.	All lessons
English language learners **communicate** information, ideas, and concepts necessary for academic success in the area of **language arts**.	All lessons

Content Area Correlations Chart

Content Area	Lessons
Reading	Thinking About Themes p. 46; Themes Across Genres p. 51; Fascinating Figures (of Speech) p. 67; Word Detective p. 99; Investigating Inferences p. 116
Writing	Perspectives on Anne Frank p. 59; Precise Prose p. 69; Making a Claim p. 88; Perfect Paragraphs p. 121
Math	Express Yourself p. 34; Variability in Pictures p. 78; Lines and Planes: Mapping Rational Numbers p. 93; Equivalent Expressions p. 109; Rad Ratios p. 126; Equivalent Numbers: One Quantity, Many Forms p. 144
Social Studies	M.A.I.N. Causes of World War I p. 29; Depression and Recession: Same or Different? p. 55; Roots of the Civil War p. 62; Revolutionary War Leaders p. 105; Women and War p. 140
Science	Water and Weather p. 40; Solar System Sculptures p. 64; Fascinating Fossils p. 83; Energy: A Case of Multiple Identities p. 135; Inquiry and Investigation p. 153

M.A.I.N. Causes of World War I

Brain-Powered Strategy	Standard
Kinesthetic Word Webs	Understands the origins and significant features of World War I

Vocabulary Words

- alliances
- assassination
- imperialism
- militarism
- nationalism

Materials

- *Title Cards* (page 31)
- *Causes Cards* (pages 32–33)
- *Causes Web* (causesweb.pdf)
- construction paper
- half-sheets of paper
- tape
- index cards
- research materials (e.g., Internet, textbooks)
- chart paper
- glue
- yarn

Preparation Note: Prior to the lesson, cut apart the *Title Cards* (page 31). Copy three sets of the *Causes Cards* (pages 32–33), and cut them apart. Additionally, on a sheet of construction paper, write *Main Topic Title Card.* You may wish to print out the causesweb.pdf from the Digital Resource CD or have students recreate it in their groups for Step 11.

Procedures

Model

1. Ask students to tell you what they know about the causes of World War I. Record their ideas on half-sheets of paper and stick them to the board using tape.

2. Have students help you rearrange the ideas into clusters based on similar topics. Guide them to identify the long-term causes of *militarism*, *alliances*, *imperialism*, and *nationalism*, and illustrate how to use the acronym M.A.I.N. to remember these causes.

3. Encourage students to identify the short-term cause of the *assassination* of Austrian Archduke Franz Ferdinand and his wife. Place the appropriate *Title Cards* above each cluster.

4. Place each *Title Card* (page 31) in the center of the board, and demonstrate how to create a web by connecting each of the five topics to the main topic by drawing lines between them.

M.A.I.N. Causes of World War I *(cont.)*

Apply/Analyze

5. Distribute the *Causes Cards* to each student. You may wish to use the enlarged versions of these cards found on the Digital Resource CD (filename: causescards.pdf). Instruct students to walk around the room and find students with cards that relate to their cards. These cards may be related words, definitions, or examples.

6. Once a group of students has found all of the related words, with no duplicates, have students form a *Kinesthetic Word Web*. (For detailed information on this strategy, see page 12.) There should be two or three separate *Kinesthetic Word Webs*, one for each set of cards.

Evaluate/Create

7. Collect the *Causes Cards* from students and remove several cards. Replace these cards with wild cards (blank index cards).

8. Repeat Steps 5–6. Have students with wild cards write an example, a definition, or a nonexample on their card and join the appropriate webs. Those with nonexamples may choose to stand near the groups for which they are nonexamples or across the room to show that they do not belong to any group.

9. Debrief with students, using the following questions:

- How did you decide which group to join or not join?

- Was it easier or harder with some of the blank cards? Why or why not?

10. Divide students into five groups and assign each group a cause from the vocabulary words listed on the previous page.

11. Have students recreate the web below on a separate sheet of paper, or you may wish to distribute copies of the *Causes Web* activity sheet found on the Digital Resource CD (filename: causesweb.pdf) to each group.

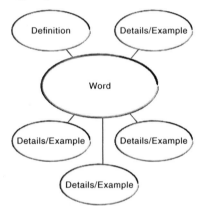

12. Ask students to research their assigned causes using their textbooks, or other provided materials. Have each group complete the web to provide more detailed information about each cause.

13. Give each group a set of index cards. Have them record the content from each oval on the *Causes Web* on separate index cards.

14. Collect the index cards and randomly redistribute them. Have students walk around and find other related cards. Stand in the middle of the classroom and hold up the construction paper titled *Main Topic Title Card*. Have students form a class *Kinesthetic Word Web* around you.

15. After creating the web, glue the *Main Topic Title Card* in the middle of a sheet of chart paper. Allow students to glue their index cards onto the paper to create visual word webs using yarn to connect the cards. Encourage students to keep adding to the webs as they learn more about the topic.

Title Cards

Teacher Directions: Cut apart the cards below.

militarism

alliances

imperialism

nationalism

assassination

Causes Cards

Teacher Directions: Copy and cut apart the cards below. Create three sets.

the belief that a country should maintain a high level of military preparedness	agreements between two or more countries to give each other help if needed	when a country takes over another country or land and makes the citizens subject to their rule	a strong feeling of national pride and a belief in the rights and interests of one's own country
militarism	**alliances**	**imperialism**	**nationalism**

Causes Cards *(cont.)*

to murder by surprise attack, often for political reasons

Archduke Franz Ferdinand, the heir to the Austrian throne, was assassinated by a Serbian rebel while visiting Sarajevo in 1914.

France and Britain had large colonial holdings in Asia and Africa that provided them with raw materials for industrialization.

The reunification of Italy in 1861 and Germany in 1871 led to strong feelings of national pride in these countries.

assassination

Major Causes of World War I

France and Germany more than doubled the size of their armies in the years leading up to World War I.

Triple Entente—Britain, Russia, and France agree to support one another to counter the increasing threat from Germany.

Express Yourself

Brain-Powered Strategy	Standard
Kinesthetic Word Webs	Identify parts of an expression using mathematical terms

Vocabulary Words

- coefficient
- expression
- operation
- variable

Materials

- *Math Term Definition* (page 36)
- *Math Term Cards* (pages 37–38)
- *Math Term Web* (mathtermweb.pdf)
- *Terms Used in Math Expressions* (page 39)
- construction paper
- dictionary or textbook glossary
- chart paper
- highlighters
- index cards

Preparation Note: Prior to the lesson, cut apart the *Math Term Cards* (pages 37–38). Additionally, on a sheet of construction paper, write *Main Topic Title Card*. You may wish to print out the mathtermweb.pdf from the Digital Resource CD or have students recreate it in their groups for Step 10.

Procedures

Model

1. Divide students into five groups, and assign each group one of the following terms: *coefficient, expression, operation, variable*.

2. Distribute the *Math Term Definition* activity sheet (page 36) to each group, and have students look up the definition of their assigned terms in a dictionary or a textbook glossary. Ask students to create examples that illustrate their terms.

3. Allow each group to share its definition and example with the class, and record the information on chart paper. Connect each word and definition to the main topic *Terms Used in Math Expressions* by drawing lines to create a visual web.

Apply/Analyze

4. Distribute a *Math Term Card* to each student. You may wish to use the enlarged versions of these cards found on the Digital Resource CD (filename: mathtermcards.pdf). Explain the *Kinesthetic Word Webs* strategy. (For detailed information on this strategy, see page 12.) Have students walk around the room and find students with cards that relate to their cards. These cards may be related words or definitions.

5. Once a group of students has found all of the related words, with no duplicates, have students form a *Kinesthetic Word Web*. There should be three separate *Kinesthetic Word Webs*, one for each set of cards.

Express Yourself *(cont.)*

6. Discuss how each web has three layers (main topic, key vocabulary, definitions).

Evaluate/Create

7. Collect all of the *Math Term Cards*. Remove several of the cards. Replace them with wild cards (blank index cards).

8. Repeat Steps 4–6. Have students with wild cards write examples, definitions, or nonexamples on their cards and join the appropriate webs. Those with nonexamples may choose to stand near the groups for which they are nonexamples or across the room to show that they do not belong at all.

9. Debrief with the following questions:

- How did you decide which group to join or not join?

- Was it easier or harder with some of the blank cards? Why or why not?

- What terms or examples can you add?

10. Using the same groups from Step 1, assign each group a different vocabulary word. Have students recreate the web below on a separate sheet of paper, or you may wish to distribute the *Math Term Web* activity sheet found on the Digital Resource CD (filename: mathtermweb.pdf) to each group. Have students complete the web as a group.

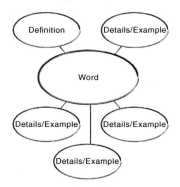

11. Distribute a set of blank index cards to each group, and ask students to record the content from each oval on their webs on separate index cards.

12. Collect all of the index cards and randomly redistribute them, one to each student. Have students walk around and find other related cards. Tape the construction paper titled *Main Topic Title Card* to a chair in the center of the room. Have students form a class *Kinesthetic Word Web* with the main topic in the center.

13. Distribute the *Terms Used in Math Expressions* activity sheet (page 39) to students. For each vocabulary word, have students create a sample mathematical example and circle or highlight the term representing each vocabulary word in the example.

14. Create a math word wall in the classroom and display the words, their definitions, and students' examples on the wall. Encourage students to add to the word wall and use it as a reference source in future lessons.

Name: _____ Date: _____

Math Term Definition

Directions: Write your assigned math term in the first box, and write the definition of the term in the middle box. In the last box, write an example of how this term is used in mathematics.

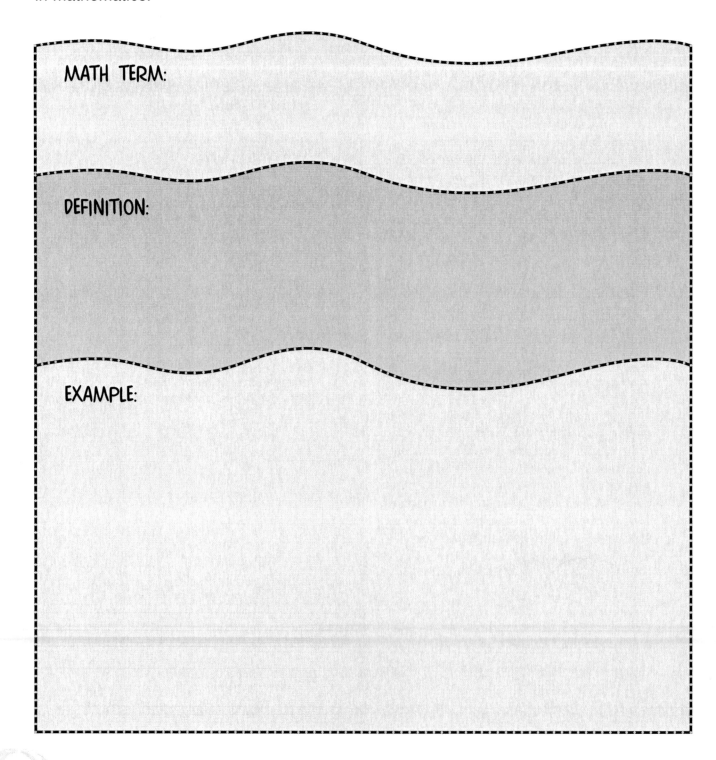

MATH TERM:

DEFINITION:

EXAMPLE:

Math Term Cards

Teacher Directions: Cut apart the cards below and randomly distribute one to each student.

numbers, symbols, and operations grouped together to show the value of something	a mathematical practice such as addition, subtraction, multiplication, and division	a symbol for an unknown number in an expression
expression	**operation**	**variable**

Math Term Cards *(cont.)*

coefficient

a number placed before a variable; it is multiplied by the variable

Terms Used in Mathematical Expressions

Name: _____ Date: _____

Terms Used in Math Expressions

Directions: For each term listed below, write two mathematical examples containing the term. Circle or highlight where each term is represented in the example.

Term	Example
expression	
operation	
variable	
coefficient	

Water and Weather

Brain-Powered Strategy	Standard
Kinesthetic Word Webs	Knows the processes involved in the water cycle and their effects on climatic patterns

Vocabulary Words

- condensation
- evaporation
- percolation
- precipitation
- surface runoff

Materials

- *Water Cycle Diagram* (page 42)
- *Water Processes Cards* (page 43)
- *Water Cycle Cards* (pages 44–45)
- *Water Cycle Word Web* (watercyclewordweb.pdf)
- large glass jar
- hot water
- plate
- ice cubes
- index cards
- butcher paper
- glue
- yarn

Preparation Note: Prior to the lesson, cut apart the *Water Processes Cards* (page 43) and the *Water Cycle Cards* (pages 44–45). You may wish to print out the watercyclewordweb.pdf from the Digital Resource CD or have students recreate it in their groups for Step 11.

Procedures

Model

1. At the front of the classroom, fill a large glass jar with about two inches of very hot water and cover the jar with a plate. Ask students to observe what is happening. Discuss the terms *evaporation* and *condensation* and how these processes relate to weather.

2. Place the ice cubes on the plate. Tell students that the cold plate represents the cold air high in the atmosphere. Observe the water condensing, and discuss *precipitation*. Review the terms *surface runoff* and *percolation* and how these processes play a role in the water cycle.

3. Distribute the *Water Cycle Diagram* activity sheet (page 42) to students, and ask them to fill in the arrows and label each process in the water cycle on the diagram.

Water and Weather *(cont.)*

4. Distribute the *Water Processes Cards* to six student volunteers. You may wish to use the enlarged versions of these cards found on the Digital Resource CD (filename: watercyclecards.pdf). Explain the *Kinesthetic Word Webs* strategy to students, and have students model the strategy using the cards. (For detailed information on this strategy, see page 12.)

Apply/Analyze

5. Distribute a *Water Cycle Card* to each student. Have students walk around the room and find students with cards that relate to their cards. These cards may be related words, definitions, or examples.

6. Once a group of students has found all of the related words, with no duplicates, have students form a *Kinesthetic Word Web* around the main topic card. Ask students how the various terms in each web relate to one another.

Evaluate/Create

7. Collect all of the *Water Cycle Cards* from students, and replace several cards with wild cards (blank index cards).

8. Have students with wild cards write an example, a definition, or a nonexample on their card. Repeat Steps 5–6. Students with nonexamples may choose to stand near the group for which they are a nonexample, or they can stand across the room to show that they do not belong to any group.

9. Debrief with students, using the following questions:
- How did you decide which group to join or not join?
- Was it easier or harder with some of the blank cards? Why or why not?
- What other terms can you add to the web?

10. Divide students into five groups, and assign each group a vocabulary word. Have students recreate the web below on a separate sheet of paper, or you may wish to distribute copies of the *Water Cycle Word Web* found on the Digital Resource CD (filename: watercyclewordweb.pdf) to each group. Have groups complete the web.

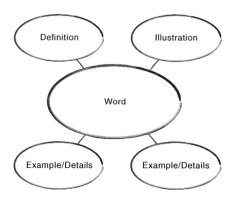

11. Distribute a set of blank index cards to each group, and ask students to record the content from each oval on their web on a separate index card. Add an additional index card with the title *Water Cycle Processes* on it.

12. Collect all of the index cards and randomly redistribute them, one to each student. Have students walk around and find other related cards. Ask the student with the *Water Cycle Processes* card to stand in the middle, and have the other students form a *Kinesthetic Word Web* around him or her.

13. Have students glue their web of index cards onto a large sheet of butcher paper. Show them how to use yarn to connect the cards to form a web. Display the web on a classroom bulletin board, and have students refer to it during future lessons.

Name: _____   Date: _____

Water Cycle Diagram

· ·

Directions: Label each part of the diagram with the appropriate water process. Draw arrows to show the movement of the water through the water cycle.

Water Processes Cards

Teacher Directions: Cut apart the cards below.

evaporation

condensation

precipitation

surface runoff

percolation

water cycle processes

Water Cycle Cards

Teacher Directions: Cut apart the cards below and randomly distribute one to each student.

evaporation	the process of converting water into vapor
condensation	the conversion of water from the vapor state to the liquid state
precipitation	the process of condensed vapor being deposited on or falling to the earth
surface runoff	water from rain or other sources that flows over the land surface

Water Cycle Cards *(cont.)*

percolation	the slow passage of a liquid (water) through a permeable substance (soil)
water cycle processes	**rain**
groundwater infiltration	**dew**
volcanic steam	**snowmelt**

Thinking About Themes

Brain-Powered Strategy	Standard
Kinesthetic Word Webs	Determine a theme or a central idea of a text and how it is conveyed through particular details; provide a summary of the text distinct from personal opinions or judgments

Vocabulary Words

- details
- judgment
- opinion
- summary
- theme

Materials

- *Three Little Pigs* (page 48)
- *Three Little Pigs Cards* (page 49)
- *Bully Cards* (page 50)
- *Theme Word Web* (themewordweb.pdf)
- *Bully* by Patricia Polacco
- index cards
- writing paper

Preparation Note: Prior to the lesson, cut apart the *Three Little Pigs Cards* (page 49). Also cut apart the *Bully Cards* (page 50). You may wish to print out the themewordweb.pdf from the Digital Resource CD or have students recreate it in their groups for Step 11.

Procedures

Model

1. Distribute the *Three Little Pigs* activity sheet (page 48) to each student. Select students to read each statement aloud. Have students note whether each statement reflects a theme, a detail, or an opinion/judgment.

2. Divide students into small groups, and have them discuss how they categorized the statements on the activity sheet. Discuss any questions or disagreements as a class.

3. Create an example word web on the board with the theme from the *Three Little Pigs* activity sheet in the middle oval and the details in the surrounding ovals. Omit the opinions/judgments from the web.

4. Distribute the *Three Little Pigs Cards* to six student volunteers. You may wish to use the enlarged versions of these cards found on the Digital Resource CD (filename: threelittlepigscards.pdf).Explain the *Kinesthetic Word Webs* strategy, and have student volunteers model a *Kinesthetic Word Web*. (For detailed information on this strategy, see page 12.)

Thinking About Themes *(cont.)*

Apply/Analyze

5. Read the story *Bully* by Patricia Polacco aloud to the class or have students read it chorally. Distribute a *Bully Card* to each student. You may wish to use the enlarged versions of these cards found on the Digital Resource CD (filename: bullycards.pdf). Have students walk around the room and find students with cards that relate to their cards.

6. Once a group of students has found all of the related words/phrases, with no duplicates, have students form a *Kinesthetic Word Web*.

7. Debrief with students, and ask them how the various terms in each web relate to one another. Identify the themes of the story and the details for each theme.

Evaluate/Create

8. Collect all of the *Bully Cards* from students, and replace several cards with wild cards (blank index cards).

9. Have students with wild cards write a theme, a detail, or an opinion/judgment on their cards. Repeat Steps 5–6. Those students with cards containing opinions or judgments should stand to the side to show that they do not belong to any group.

10. Debrief with students, using the following questions:

- How did you decide which group to join or not join?

- Was it easier or harder with some of the blank cards? Why or why not?

- What other words or phrases could you add to the web?

11. Divide students into four groups, and assign each group one of the following key ideas: *bully, cyber-bullying, friendship, cliques.* Have students recreate the web below on a separate sheet of paper, or you may wish to distribute copies of the *Theme Word Web* activity sheet found on the Digital Resource CD (filename: themewordweb.pdf) to each group. Have students complete the web as a group.

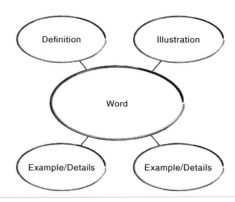

12. Give each group a set of index cards, and ask students to record the content from each oval on their webs on a separate index card.

13. Collect all of the index cards, and randomly redistribute them, one to each student. Have students walk around and find other related cards. Once a group is complete, have them form a *Kinesthetic Word Web* with the key idea, or theme, in the middle and the related details around the outside.

14. Distribute writing paper to students. Have each student write a summary paragraph reviewing the key ideas and details from the story *Bully*. Remind students that a text summary should not include opinions or judgments about the story. Have students share their paragraphs with a partner.

Name: _____   Date: _____

Three Little Pigs

. . . .

Directions: Read each statement and label whether it represents a theme (*T*), a detail (*D*), or an opinion (*O*).

Statement	Type
The Three Little Pigs is the best story to read to young children.	
The first little pig quickly builds a house out of straw.	
Hard work and patience pays off in the end.	
The second little pig hastily builds his house out of sticks.	
The third little pig works slowly and carefully to build a secure house out of bricks.	
Laziness leads to failure.	
The Big Bad Wolf blows down the first two pigs' houses, but he cannot blow down the third pig's house of bricks.	
The first two little pigs should spend more time on their houses and choose stronger building materials.	

Three Little Pigs Cards

Teacher Directions: Cut apart the cards below.

Hard work and patience pays off in the end.

The first two little pigs build their houses quickly out of straw and sticks.

The third little pig takes his time and works hard to construct a house made out of bricks.

The wolf is able to blow over the houses made of straw and sticks.

The first two little pigs run to the third little pig's house to hide from the wolf.

The wolf is not able to blow down the third little pig's house of bricks.

Bully Cards

Teacher Directions: Cut apart the cards below and randomly distribute one to each student.

Bullying	Gage, Kenyon, and Maeve feel powerful because they exclude people from their clique.
Bullies exclude people as a way to gain power.	Lyla changes her physical appearance and mannerisms to be more like the "popular" girls.
Bullies want to control and manipulate people.	Gage, Kenyon, and Maeve make fun of other students in order to feel better about themselves.
Bullies put down other people as a way of making themselves feel more powerful and secure.	Lyla feels special when Gage, Kenyon, and Maeve invite her to be friends with them.

Themes Across Genres

Brain-Powered Strategy	Standard
It Takes Two	Compare and contrast texts in different forms or genres in terms of their approaches to similar themes and topics

Vocabulary Words

- compare
- contrast
- genre
- theme

Materials

- *Comparing Themes* (page 53)
- *Our Feedback* (page 54)
- *Wonder* by A. J. Palacio
- sticky notes (two colors; several pads)
- "The Man in the Iron Pail Mask" by Shel Silverstein

Preparation Note: Prior to the lesson, have students read the novel *Wonder* by A. J. Palacio over an extended time period, or select a short excerpt for them to read in class.

Procedures

Model

1. Create a two-column T-chart on the board labeled *Similarities* and *Differences,* with the title *Poetry and Fictional Literature* at the top. Explain the *It Takes Two* strategy to students. (For detailed information on this strategy, see page 13.)

2. Ask students to brainstorm similarities and differences between fictional literature and poetry. Record their ideas on sticky notes, and stick them to the T-chart in the appropriate column.

3. Discuss the chart with the class, and assess whether all of the sticky notes were placed in the correct column.

4. Model how to use sticky notes of a different color to write constructive comments, questions, or suggestions about the ideas on the chart.

Themes Across Genres *(cont.)*

Apply/Analyze

5. Distribute copies of "The Man in the Iron Pail Mask" by Shel Silverstein to students. Instruct students to read the poem independently, and then ask for a volunteer to read the poem aloud to the class. Discuss the theme of the poem, and as a class take notes on the theme by creating a word web such as the following:

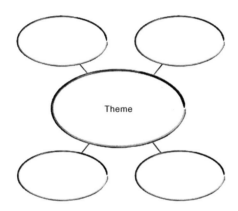

6. Divide students into small groups. Ask students to discuss how the novel *Wonder* by A. J. Palacio relates to "The Man in the Iron Pail Mask" by Shel Silverstein.

7. Distribute copies of the *Comparing Themes* activity sheet (page 53) to each group, as well as a stack of sticky notes. Have students use the *It Takes Two* strategy to record the similarities and differences between the poem and the novel.

Evaluate/Create

8. Ask students to leave their *Comparing Themes* activity sheets on their desks. Distribute the *Our Feedback* activity sheet (page 54) to students. Have students rotate around the classroom, discussing each group's chart, and completing an *Our Feedback* activity sheet to leave for the group. Ask students to consider the following questions:

- Do you agree or disagree with your classmates' choices?

- Are there any changes you would make?

In addition to completing the *Our Feedback* activity sheet, students may also record their suggestions and/or disagreements on different color sticky notes that can be directly affixed to the group's comparison chart.

9. Allow the groups to review the feedback provided on the *Our Feedback* activity sheets and make revisions as necessary.

10. After reviewing and incorporating the feedback, ask each student to write an essay comparing and contrasting the themes presented in the two texts.

Name: _____ Date: _____

Comparing Themes

· ·

Directions: Write the names of the poem and the novel on the lines at the top of the chart. On sticky notes, write your ideas. Place each sticky note in the appropriate column.

_____ and _____

Similarities	Differences

Name: _____ Date: _____

Our Feedback

Directions: Discuss another group's chart. Record your responses below.

**What We Agree With,
and Why**

**What We Disagree With,
and Why**

Depression and Recession: Same or Different?

Brain-Powered Strategy	Standard
It Takes Two	Understands the causes of the Great Depression and how it affected American society

Vocabulary Words

- Great Depression
- recession
- shantytown
- sharecropper

Materials

- *Note Sheet* (page 57)
- *Comparing Themes* (page 58)
- *Our Feedback* (page 54)
- Depression-era photograph of impoverished sharecroppers
- Depression-era photograph of urban shantytown
- sticky notes (several pads; two different colors)
- two different newspaper articles on the Great Depression
- two different newspaper articles on the recent recession

Preparation Note: Collect newspaper articles on the Great Depression and our recent recession. Additionally, collect photographs on impoverished sharecroppers and urban shantytowns from the depression era. You may wish to use the pictures available on the Digital Resource CD (filename: depressioneraimages.pdf).

Procedures

Model

1. Display the Great Depression photographs. Ask students to observe the similarities and differences between the two.

2. Create a two-column T-chart on the board labeled *Similarities* and *Differences*. Explain the *It Takes Two* strategy to students. (For detailed information on this strategy, see page 13.) Record their observations about the photographs on sticky notes, and stick them to the T-chart in the appropriate column.

3. Discuss the chart with the class, and assess whether all of the sticky notes were placed in the correct column.

4. Model how to use sticky notes of a different color to write constructive comments, questions, or suggestions about the ideas on the chart.

Depression and Recession: Same or Different? *(cont.)*

Apply/Analyze

5. Divide students into groups of four. Distribute the *Note Sheet* activity sheet (page 57) to students. Provide each group with four newspaper articles—two articles on the Great Depression and two articles on the recent economic recession. Ask each student to choose an article to read, and instruct students to use the *Note Sheet* activity sheet to take notes on their selected article as they read it.

6. Have students share their notes from the article with the rest of the students in the group.

7. Distribute the *Comparing Themes* activity sheet (page 58) and a stack of sticky notes (one color) to each group. Have students use the *It Takes Two* strategy to record the similarities and differences between these two periods of economic turmoil.

Evaluate/Create

8. Ask students to leave their *Comparing Themes* activity sheets on their desks. Distribute the *Our Feedback* activity sheet (page 54) to students. Have students rotate around the classroom, discussing each group's chart and completing an *Our Feedback* activity sheet to leave for the group. Ask students to consider the following questions:

- Do you agree or disagree with your classmates' choices?

- Are there any changes you would make?

In addition to completing the *Our Feedback* activity sheet, students may also record their suggestions and/or disagreements on different color sticky notes that can be directly affixed to the group's comparison chart.

9. Allow the groups to review the feedback provided on the *Our Feedback* activity sheets and make revisions as necessary.

10. In their groups, have students write questions for mock television interviews relating the recent recession to the Great Depression. Instruct students to take turns pretending to be reporters and the "leading economic consultants" being interviewed. If possible, videotape the interviews.

Name: _____   Date: _____

Note Sheet

· ·

Directions: Take notes on your newspaper article, using the categories below.

Event

Causes

Economic Effects

Societal Effects

Name: _____   Date: _____

Comparing Themes

Directions: Write the names of the two events you will be comparing on the lines below. On sticky notes, write your ideas. Place each sticky note in the appropriate column.

_____ and _____

Similarities	Differences

Perspectives on Anne Frank

Brain-Powered Strategy	Standard
It Takes Two	Compare and contrast one author's presentation of events with that of another

Vocabulary Words

- deportation
- fascism
- Holocaust
- scapegoat

Materials

- *Comparing the Anne Frank Experience* (page 61)
- *Our Feedback* (page 54)
- writing paper
- sticky notes (several pads; two different colors)
- reading selection from *A Diary of a Young Girl* by Anne Frank
- reading selection from *Anne Frank Remembered: The Story of the Woman Who Helped to Hide the Frank Family* by Miep Gies

Procedures

Model

1. Review the story of Anne Frank and the situation her family faced when they went into hiding in Amsterdam during World War II.

2. Divide the class in half. Distribute writing paper, and ask half of the class to write a paragraph from the Franks' perspective on how it felt to go into hiding from the Nazis. Have the other half of the class write a paragraph from the perspective of Miep Gies, the secretary who hid the Frank family, on how it felt to illegally shelter the Frank family.

3. Create a two-column T-chart on the board labeled *Similarities* and *Differences*. Explain the *It Takes Two* strategy to students. (For detailed information on this strategy, see page 13.)

4. Assign partners to students, one from each half of the class, so that both perspectives are represented. Instruct students to switch paragraphs and read one another's writing.

5. As a class, complete the T-chart on the board comparing the two different perspectives using the *It Takes Two* strategy.

Perspectives on Anne Frank *(cont.)*

Apply/Analyze

6. Divide students into groups of four. Give two students in the group a reading selection from *The Diary of a Young Girl* by Anne Frank. Provide the other two students in the group with a selection from *Anne Frank Remembered: The Story of the Woman Who Helped to Hide the Frank Family* by Miep Gies. Have students read their selections.

7. Ask students in each group to take turns reviewing their reading selection with the other group members. Encourage students to explicitly reference the text and highlight important themes and concepts in each piece.

8. Distribute the *Comparing the Anne Frank Experience* activity sheet (page 61) and a stack of sticky notes to each group. Ask students to use the *It Takes Two* strategy to record the similarities and differences between the two perspectives presented in the reading selections.

Evaluate/Create

9. Instruct students to leave their *Comparing the Anne Frank Experience* activity sheets on their desks. Distribute the *Our Feedback* activity sheet (page 54) to each group. Have students rotate around the classroom, discussing each group's chart and completing the *Our Feedback* activity sheet to leave for the group. Ask students to consider the following questions:

- Do you agree or disagree with your classmates' choices?

- Are there any changes you would make?

Students may also record their suggestions and/or disagreements on different color sticky notes that can be directly stuck to the group's comparison chart.

10. Allow the groups to review the feedback provided on the *Our Feedback* activity sheets and make revisions as necessary.

11. Have students write diary entries about the Holocaust from the following perspectives: American soldier, German soldier, and German Jewish child. Discuss as a class how an author's perspective can influence the portrayal of historical events.

Name: _____ Date: _____

Comparing the Anne Frank Experience

· ·

Directions: Write the names of the two perspectives you will be comparing on the lines below. On sticky notes, write your ideas. Place each sticky note in the appropriate column.

_____ and _____

Similarities	Differences

Roots of the Civil War

Brain-Powered Strategy	Standard
Show It with Dough!	Understands the causes of the Civil War

Vocabulary Words

- abolitionist
- agricultural economy
- industrial economy
- slavery

Materials

- *No-Cook Dough Recipe* (doughrecipe.pdf)
- chart paper
- passage from a book about slavery (e.g., *Letters from a Slave Girl: The Story of Harriet Jacobs* by Mary E. Lyons)
- file folders
- index cards

Preparation Note: Prior to the lesson, create molding dough for students, using the *No-Cook Dough Recipe* found on the Digital Resource CD (filename: doughrecipe.pdf). Recreate the web shown in Step 2 on chart paper.

Procedures

Model

1. Read the selected literature passage to students describing life as a slave on a southern plantation before the Civil War.

2. Recreate the web below on a sheet of chart paper for students to see. Have students brainstorm what they know about the topic, and record their answers on the web. Discuss the causes, adding additional ones if necessary, and familiarize students with the vocabulary words listed above.

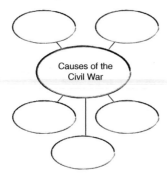

3. Explain the *Show It with Dough!* strategy to students. (For detailed information on this strategy, see page 14.) Ask students to watch as you model something out of dough without telling them what it is. For example, you might model a cotton ball as a way to represent the agricultural economy of the South.

4. Instruct students to turn to classmates and share what they think you made. Have them consider what they would have added to your sculpture, and why.

Roots of the Civil War *(cont.)*

Apply/Analyze

5. Provide each student with some molding dough and a file folder. Show students how to create their own "studio" by standing their file folders on end to create privacy.

6. Give students several minutes to use the *Show It with Dough!* strategy to create sculptures representing one of the causes of the Civil War. Instruct students to keep their work private and not discuss or share it during this time.

7. Distribute index cards to students, and have them place the cards in front of their sculptures. Have students stand up, leaving their sculptures on their desks, and rotate to a different desk.

8. Ask students to observe the work on the desks. Give students 15 seconds to record notes on the index cards about what they see.

9. Have students rotate again. Give students 30 seconds to read the other notes on the index cards and add more details. Tell students that they may not repeat any details already listed. Guide them to make observations about the texture, shape, lines, etc., of the sculpture.

10. Continue rotating for 30 seconds until at least five students have commented on each sculpture.

Evaluate/Create

11. Have students return to their own desks. Have them answer the following questions:

- Is there enough detail to tell what your sculpture represents? If not, what can you add?

- How does your sculpture relate to the topic of study?

12. Using the same partners from Step 4, tell students to reveal what their sculpture represents and how it relates to the topic of study. Ask for several volunteers to share their sculptures with the class.

13. Discuss the importance of adding details in both writing and art. Explain that details help to make our ideas clearer and also make the work more interesting. Using the ideas written on their index cards, ask students to add more details to their sculptures.

14. Distribute additional index cards to students, and have them write their names and explanations of their work. Ask students to group their sculptures by theme (e.g., slavery, economics, social differences) and create an "art gallery" by displaying the sculptures, along with the explanation cards, around the classroom. Invite another class to come visit the gallery to learn more about the causes of the Civil War.

Solar System Sculptures

Brain-Powered Strategy	**Standard**
Show It with Dough!	Knows characteristics and movement patterns of the planets in our Solar System

Vocabulary Words	**Materials**
• composition • elliptical orbits • planets • solar system	• *No-Cook Dough Recipe* (doughrecipe.pdf) • *Solar System Diagram* (page 66) • index cards • model or poster showing the planets in our solar system • file folders

Preparation Note: Prior to the lesson, create molding dough for students, using the *No-Cook Dough Recipe* found on the Digital Resource CD (filename: doughrecipe.pdf).

Procedures

Model

1. Distribute eight index cards to each student. Display a model or poster depicting the planets in our solar system. Review the characteristics of each planet and the movement patterns of their orbits. Model for students how to take notes using each index card to reflect each planet.

2. Discuss the *Show It with Dough!* strategy with students. (For detailed information on this strategy, see page 14.) Without telling students what you are creating, model something out of dough that represents a feature of the solar system. For example, a planet could be made out of a ball of dough.

3. Instruct students to turn to a partner and share what they think you made. Ask them to consider the following questions:

   • What do you think the sculpture represents?

   • How is this topic relevant to the unit of study?

   • What would you add to the sculpture? Why?

Solar System Sculptures *(cont.)*

Apply/Analyze

4. Provide each student with some molding dough and a file folder. Show students how to stand their file folders on end to create private work space.

5. Ask students to use the *Show It with Dough!* strategy to create a sculpture representing a feature of the solar system. Tell students to work independently and refrain from sharing their work with their classmates.

6. Place an index card in front of each sculpture and have students stand up, leaving their sculptures on their desks, and rotate to a different desk.

7. Give students 15 seconds to observe the sculptures on the desks and record notes about what they see on the index card.

8. Have students rotate again. This time, give students 30 seconds to read the other notes on the index cards and add more details. Encourage students not to repeat any details already listed. If necessary, demonstrate how to examine a sculpture by thinking aloud about the shape, texture, lines, etc., of the sculpture.

9. Continue rotating for 30 seconds until at least five students have commented on each sculpture.

Evaluate/Create

10. Have students return to their own desks and think about the following questions:

- Is there enough detail to tell what your sculpture represents? If not, what can you add?

- How does your sculpture relate to the topic of study?

11. Divide students into small groups of four or five students. Arrange students' desks in a circle, and have students take turns sharing their sculpture and revealing what it represents. Ask students to relate their sculptures to the main topic of the solar system.

12. Discuss the importance and purpose of adding details to enhance understanding. Have students add more details to their sculptures using the suggestions from the index cards.

13. Give students an additional index card, and have them write their name and an explanation of their work on the card.

14. Assign students a partner. Distribute the *Solar System Diagram* activity sheet (page 66) to pairs, and have student pairs record relevant information about the different planets in our solar system and additional notes about the topic. Allow students to circulate around the room and examine their classmates' sculptures and explanations to aid in their completion of the activity sheet.

Name: _____ Date: _____

Solar System Diagram

· ·

Directions: Label each planet in the diagram. Record several important characteristics about each of the planets in the adjacent box. List additional information you know about our solar system on the lines at the bottom of the page.

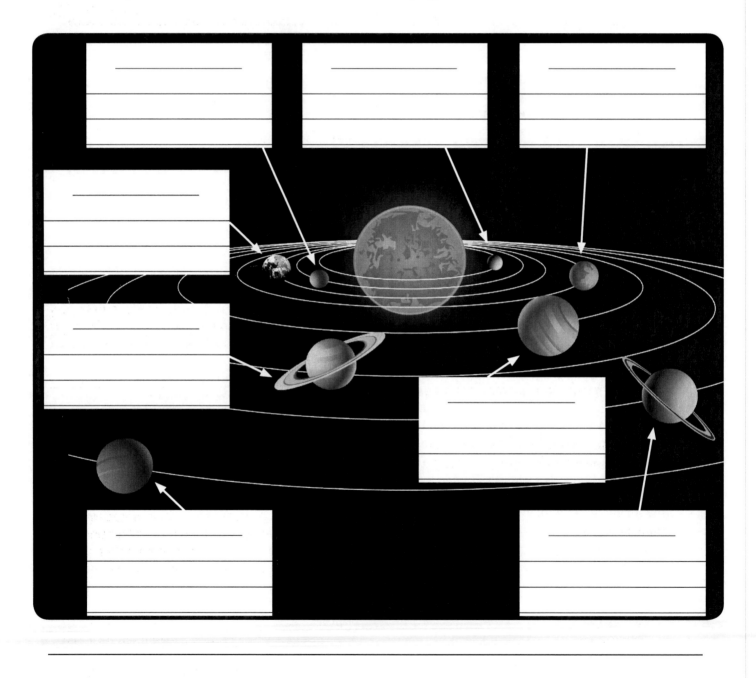

_____

_____

_____

Fascinating Figures (of Speech)

Brain-Powered Strategy	**Standard**
Show It with Dough!	Determine the meaning of words and phrases as they are used in a text, including figurative and connotative meanings

Vocabulary Words	**Materials**
• hyperbole • idiom • metaphor • personification • simile	• *No-Cook Dough Recipe* (doughrecipe.pdf) • "Sick" by Shel Silverstein • *Quick as a Cricket* by Audrey Wood and Don Wood • file folders • timer • index cards • colored pencils • drawing paper

Preparation Note: Prior to the lesson, create molding dough for students, using the *No-Cook Dough Recipe* found on the Digital Resource CD (filename: doughrecipe.pdf).

Procedures

Model

1. Read the poem "Sick" by Shel Silverstein and the picture book *Quick as a Cricket* by Audrey Wood and Don Wood. Discuss the use of similes in the poem and book.

2. Explain the term *figurative language*. Have students brainstorm different types of figurative language, such as *hyperbole*, *idiom*, *metaphor*, *personification*, and *simile*, and brainstorm examples for each different type. Record their ideas on the board.

3. Discuss the *Show It with Dough!* strategy with students. (For detailed information on this strategy, see page 14.) Without telling students what you are creating, model something out of dough that represents something related to figurative language. For example, molding a horse onto a plate could depict the hyperbole *I'm so hungry I could eat a horse.*

4. Ask students to guess what they think your sculpture represents. Have them turn to a partner and share their ideas. Reveal what you made and how it relates to figurative language. Have the partners discuss what they would have added to your sculpture, and why.

Fascinating Figures (of Speech) *(cont.)*

Apply/Analyze

5. Provide each student with some molding dough and a file folder. Demonstrate how to stand the file folder on end to create a private workspace.

6. Review the different types of figurative language and the examples from Step 2. Have students use the *Show It with Dough!* strategy to create a sculpture representing the concept of figurative language. Encourage students to work independently and refrain from looking at their peers' work.

7. Distribute an index card to each student and instruct students to place the cards in front of their sculptures. Leaving their sculptures on their desks, have students rotate to the left so they are standing in front of a new desk.

8. Tell students to observe the sculptures on the desks and record notes about what they see on the index cards. Set a timer for 15 seconds to complete this task.

9. Have students rotate again. Give students 30 seconds to read the other notes on the index card and add more details. Encourage students not to repeat any details already listed.

10. Continue rotating for 30 seconds until at least five students have commented on each sculpture.

Evaluate/Create

11. Have students return to their own desks and evaluate their sculptures, using the following questions:

- Is there enough detail to tell what your sculpture represents? If not, what can you add?

- How does your sculpture relate to the topic of study?

12. Discuss how details can enhance understanding and interest in a piece of writing or art. Ask students to add more details to their sculptures using the suggestions from the index cards.

13. Distribute drawing paper to each student. Have students draw a visual representation of their sculpture on the page. Underneath their drawing, have them reveal what their depiction represents and how it relates to the topic of figurative language.

14. Collect the pages, and staple them together to form a classroom book.

Precise Prose

Brain-Powered Strategy	Standard
I'm in the Pic	Use precise language and domain-specific vocabulary to inform about or explain the topic

Vocabulary Words

- auditory
- olfactory
- precise language
- tactile
- visual

Materials

- *Descriptive Language Sentences* (page 71)
- *Descriptive Language Practice* (page 72)
- *I'm in the Pic* (pages 73–74)
- *Thinking About Pictures* (pages 75–76)
- *Creating My Own Picture* (page 77)
- detailed pictures
- chart paper or sentence strips containing question stems
- pictures showing kids or students

Procedures

Model

1. Read the sentences from the *Descriptive Language Sentences* activity sheet (page 71) to students one at a time in order. After reading each sentence, pause and ask a student to explain what detail was added that was not in the previous sentence.

2. Distribute a *Descriptive Language Practice* activity sheet (page 72) to each student. Have them practice writing sentences with descriptive language about a topic of their choosing.

3. Explain the *I'm in the Pic* strategy to students. (For detailed information on this strategy, see page 15.) Discuss how the use of precise language in writing allows the reader to understand and experience the text more fully.

4. Discuss the five senses and introduce the associated words: *visual*, *auditory*, *tactile*, and *olfactory*. Show students a picture with lots of detail from a book. Ask students the following questions: If you were in this picture...

   - What might you see?
   - What might you touch?
   - What might you hear?
   - What could you smell?
   - Do you think you could taste anything?
   - What emotions do you think you might feel if you were there in the picture?

Precise Prose *(cont.)*

5. Post question stems, including higher-level questions such as *What if...* or *I wonder...* and model using them as you think aloud about the picture. Ask students to turn to partners and ask questions about the picture.

Apply/Analyze

6. Assign students partners, and distribute an *I'm in the Pic* activity sheet (pages 73–74) and a detailed picture to each student pair. Allow students to complete the activity sheet with their partners.

7. Have each pair of students trade pictures and activity sheets with another pair. Instruct students to examine the new picture and then read the description on the *I'm in the Pic* activity sheet. Have students underline examples of precise language in the description and then trade back.

Evaluate/Create

8. Provide students with an assortment of pictures showing students or kids in a variety of environments. Distribute the *Thinking About Pictures* activity sheet (pages 75–76). Have each student pick a picture and complete the activity sheet independently. Remind students about the importance of using precise language.

9. Ask for volunteers to share their work with the class. Point out examples of precise language in the students' work.

10. Tell students to think of a situation or experience that was particularly vivid for them. Distribute the *Creating My Own Picture* activity sheet (page 77) to students. Have students draw pictures of their chosen experiences and write explanations. Encourage students to use precise language and address at least one of the questions on the activity sheet in their explanations.

11. Display students' pictures and explanations on a bulletin board. Encourage students to examine their classmates' work and respond to what they see and read.

Descriptive Language Sentences

Teacher Directions: Read the sentences below one at a time. After reading each sentence, pause and ask students to identify the additional detail that was not present in the previous sentence.

1. I licked my ice cream cone.

2. I licked my chocolate ice cream cone.

3. I licked my chocolate ice cream cone as it started to drip.

4. I quickly licked my chocolate ice cream cone as it started to drip.

5. I quickly licked my chocolate ice cream cone as it started to drip down my wrist.

6. I quickly licked my chocolate ice cream cone as it started to drip down my wrist and onto my shirt.

7. I quickly licked my towering chocolate ice cream cone as it started to drip down my wrist and onto my shirt.

8. I quickly licked my towering chocolate ice cream cone as it started to drip down my wrist and onto my shirt in the hot, humid weather.

Name: _____   Date: _____

Descriptive Language Practice

Directions: Think of a personal experience or a topic that you can describe in detail. Start by writing a basic sentence about the topic on the first line. On each subsequent line, add one detail to the original sentence to describe the experience or topic with more precise language.

Original Sentence

_____

_____

Detailed Sentence 1

_____

_____

Detailed Sentence 2

_____

_____

Detailed Sentence 3

_____

_____

Name: _____ Date: _____

I'm in the Pic

Directions: Look at a picture. Write or draw details from the picture in each box.

I'm in the Picture!	I smell...
I see...	I taste...
I hear...	I touch...

#51183—Brain-Powered Lessons to Engage All Learners

Name: _____   Date: _____

I'm in the Pic *(cont.)*

Directions: Write about or draw how you might feel if you were in the picture. Explain why.

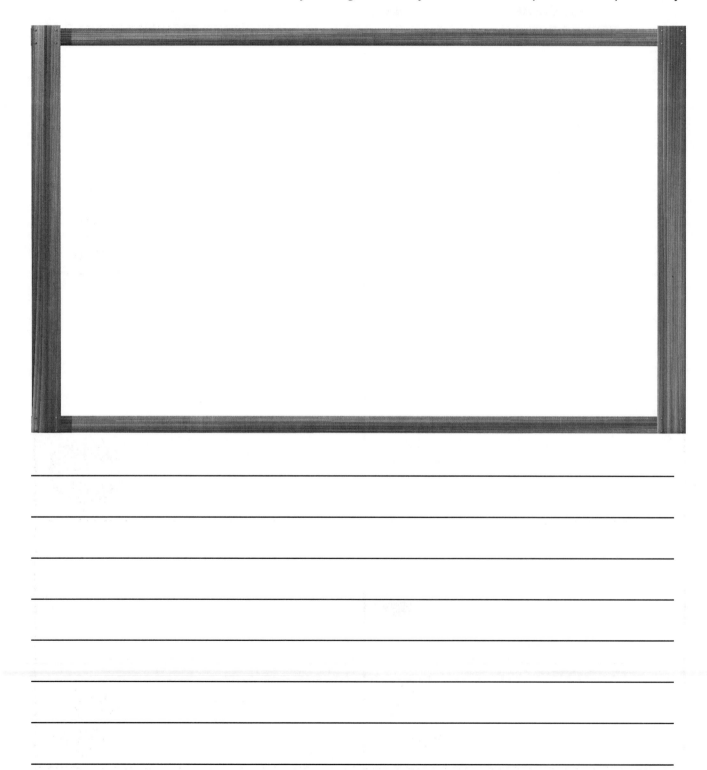

_____

_____

_____

_____

_____

_____

_____

Name: _____ Date: _____

Thinking About Pictures

Directions: Look at a picture. Write or draw details from the picture in each box.

I'm in the Picture!	I smell...
I see...	I taste...
I hear...	I touch...

Name: _____ Date: _____

Thinking About Pictures *(cont.)*

....

Directions: Look at the picture you chose and answer the questions below.

1. How would you feel if you were in the picture?

_____

_____

_____

_____

2. What information can you use to support your answer to Question 1?

_____

_____

_____

_____

3. What is your opinion of what you see and know about the picture?

_____

_____

_____

_____

Name: _____ Date: _____

Creating My Own Picture

Directions: Create your own picture, using what you know about the topic of study and/or new questions you have.

Directions: Write an explanation about your picture on a separate sheet of paper. Be sure to include responses for the questions below.

a. How can you connect your picture with something you learned about precise language?

b. Can you connect your illustration to something you have learned before about the topic or in another area of study?

c. In what way would you design or reinvent something you learned about the topic of study?

Variability in Pictures

Brain-Powered Strategy	Standard
I'm in the Pic	Recognize a statistical question as one that anticipates variability in the data related to the question and accounts for it in the answers

Vocabulary Words

- center
- distribution
- spread
- statistical question
- variability

Materials

- *Height Chart Data* (page 80)
- *I'm in the Pic* (page 73–74)
- *Thinking About Pictures* (page 81)
- *Creating My Own Picture* (page 82)
- measuring tapes
- assortment of pictures showing one individual and groups of items (e.g., people, plants, animals, buildings)

Preparation Note: Collect various pictures, including one of a single person and one of a group of items, specifically people.

Procedures

Model

1. Display the picture of a single person. Ask the class, "How tall is this person?" Record students' estimates, and discuss how there is a single answer to this question because there is no variability.

2. Show students the picture of multiple people and ask them, "How tall are these people?" Discuss how this is a statistical question because the people in the picture are different heights. You may also wish to discuss the vocabulary words at this time.

3. Distribute the *Height Chart Data* activity sheet (page 80), and guide students to work with partners to graph data on the dot plot and find the center and spread of the distribution. Discuss how this data accounts for the variability in heights.

4. Explain the *I'm in the Pic* strategy to students. (For detailed information on this strategy, see page 15.) Show students a picture of a crowd of people and ask them to imagine they were in the picture. Have them consider the following questions: If you were in this picture...

   - What might you see?
   - What might you touch?
   - What might you hear?
   - What could you smell?
   - Do you think you could taste anything?
   - What emotions might you feel?

Variability in Pictures *(cont.)*

5. Post question stems, including higher-level questions such as, *What if...* or *I wonder...*, and model using them as you think aloud about the picture. Include mathematical questions, such as *Are there more _____ or _____?* and *What is the average _____?* Have students identify which questions are statistical questions. Ask students to turn to their partners and ask questions about the picture.

Apply/Analyze

6. Distribute an *I'm in the Pic* activity sheet (pages 73–74) to each student pair, and a copy of a picture of a crowd of people. Allow students to complete the activity sheet with their partners.

7. Distribute a *Height Chart Data* activity sheet (page 80) to each student pair. Have students work together to measure their own heights, using a measuring tape. Ask them to add their personal height information to the chart and then graph the data.

Evaluate/Create

8. Provide students with a variety of pictures showing groups of items. Have each student pick a picture and complete the *Thinking About Pictures* activity sheet (page 81) independently.

9. Ask students to switch pictures and question sheets with a partner. Have students examine the pictures and answer the questions written by their partners. Have students switch back and discuss the answers to the questions with their partners.

10. Distribute the *Creating My Own Picture* activity sheet (page 82) to students. Ask students to create a picture that can be used to ask and answer statistical questions. Have students write a statistical question and a non-statistical question about their pictures. Have them record explanations of their pictures.

11. Make copies of the top half of the students' *Creating My Own Picture* activity sheets. Randomly distribute one sheet to each student. Have students describe why one question is considered a statistical question while the other is not.

I'm in the Pic

Name: _____   Date: _____

Height Chart Data

Directions: Write your names and heights on the bottom two rows. Use the data to complete the dot plot at the bottom of the page.

Name	Height
Susan	4'9"
Raul	5'0"
Tim	5'2"
Kiara	4'6"
Amy	4'5"
Adrianna	4'9"
Reehan	4'11"
Derrick	5'2"
Omar	4'9"
Ann	4'11"

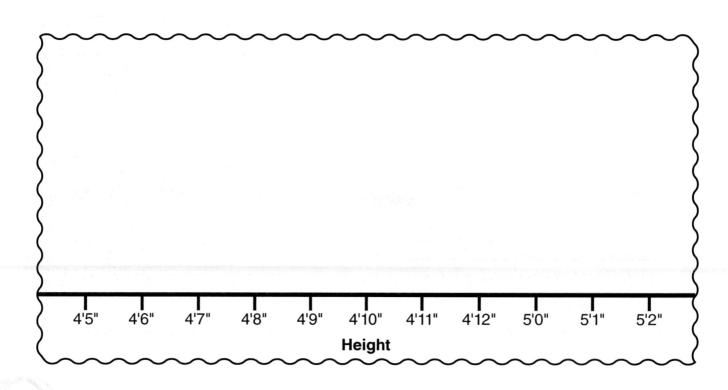

4'5" 4'6" 4'7" 4'8" 4'9" 4'10" 4'11" 4'12" 5'0" 5'1" 5'2"

Height

Name: _____ Date: _____

Thinking About Pictures

Directions: Using the picture you chose, write three statistical questions addressing the variability found in the picture.

Question #1: _____

_____

_____

Answer: _____

Question #2: _____

_____

_____

Answer: _____

Question #3: _____

_____

_____

Answer: _____

Name: _____   Date: _____

Creating My Own Picture

Directions: Create your own picture using what you know about the topic of study and/or new questions you have. Then, write a statistical question and a non-statistical question relating to your picture.

Statistical Question:

_____

_____

_____

Non-statistical Question:

_____

_____

_____

Directions: Write an explanation about your picture on a separate sheet of paper. Be sure to include responses for the questions below.

a. How can you connect your picture to something you learned about statistical variability?

b. How can pictures be helpful in understanding mathematical concepts?

c. Was it beneficial to imagine yourself as part of the picture? Why, or why not?

Fascinating Fossils

Brain-Powered Strategy	Standard
I'm in the Pic	Knows that the fossil record, through geologic evidence, documents the appearance, diversification, and extinction of many life forms

Vocabulary Words

- diversification
- evolution
- extinction
- fossil record
- geologic evidence

Materials

- *Life as an Archaeologist* (page 85)
- *I'm in the Pic* (pages 73–74)
- *Thinking About Pictures* (page 86)
- *Creating My Own Picture* (page 87)
- text selection from book on fossils and archaeological digs (e.g., *Desert Days: My Life As a Field Archaeologist* by Fred Wendorf)
- picture of an archaeology dig with fossils
- assortment of fossil pictures
- index cards

Preparation Note: Prior to the lesson, select a text passage from a book about fossils or archaeological digs that can be read aloud to the class. Collect images on various fossils, including an image of an archaeological dig with fossils.

Procedures

Model

1. Have students think about what it would be like to be archaeologists working on important archaeological digs for fossils. Distribute the *Life as an Archaeologist* activity sheet (page 85) to students.

2. Read the text selection aloud to the class, and have students take notes.

3. Explain the *I'm in the Pic* strategy to students. (For detailed information on this strategy, see page 15.) Show them a detailed photograph from the book. Have them consider the following questions: If you were in this picture...

   - What might you see?
   - What might you touch?
   - What might you hear?
   - What could you smell?
   - Do you think you could taste anything?
   - What emotions might you feel?

Fascinating Fossils *(cont.)*

Apply/Analyze

4. Post question stems, including higher-level questions such as, "What if..." or "I wonder...," and model using them as you think aloud about the picture. Ask students to turn to partners and ask questions about the picture.

5. Divide students into small groups and distribute the *I'm in the Pic* activity sheet (pages 73–74) to students, and distribute an archaeology dig image to each group. Allow students to complete the activity sheet with their groups.

6. Discuss the importance of fossils in the study of biology. Explain how fossils contribute to our knowledge of *diversification*, *evolution*, and *extinction*. Using their notes from the *Life as an Archaeologist* activity sheet and the *I'm in the Pic* activity sheet, discuss the challenges and rewards of archaeology.

Evaluate/Create

7. Provide students with a variety of pictures showing different types of fossils. Distribute the *Thinking About Pictures* activity sheet (page 86) to students. Have each student pick a picture and complete the activity sheet independently.

8. Have students share their work with partners and discuss the similarities and differences between their pictures.

9. Distribute the *Creating My Own Picture* activity sheet (page 87) to students. Ask students to create a picture using their new knowledge about fossils and/or questions they have. At the bottom, have them record an explanation of their picture.

10. Display students' pictures and explanations around the classroom. Distribute a small stack of index cards to each student. Instruct students to walk around the classroom and examine their classmates' illustrations and explanations. For each piece, have students write comments and questions on index cards and leave it by the picture.

11. Provide students time to review and respond to the questions and comments about their work.

Name: _____   Date: _____

Life as an Archaeologist

Directions: Imagine that you are an archaeologist participating in a fossil dig. Take notes on the questions below as you listen to the text passage.

What is the lifestyle of an archaeologist like?

What would be your favorite part about being an archaeologist?

What would be your least favorite part about being an archaeologist?

Why are archaeologists important? What can they teach us?

Name: _____ Date: _____

Thinking About Pictures

··

Directions: Using the picture you chose, answer at least two of the questions below.

1. How would you feel if you were in the picture?

_____

_____

_____

2. What does the information from the picture tell you about the life and work of an archaeologist?

_____

_____

_____

3. What knowledge and thoughts do you have about the picture?

_____

_____

_____

_____

Name: _____ Date: _____

Creating My Own Picture

Directions: Create your own picture, using what you know about the topic of study and/or new questions you have.

Directions: Write an explanation about your picture on a separate sheet of paper. Be sure to include responses for the questions below.

a. How can you connect your illustration to something you learned about fossils?

b. How can you connect your illustration to something you have learned before or in another related area?

c. How could you expand your illustration to show more information about fossils?

Making a Claim

Brain-Powered Strategy	Standard
Response Cards	Write arguments to support claims with clear reasons and relevant evidence

Vocabulary Words	Materials
• claim • counterclaim • evidence • reason	• *Making a Claim* (page 90) • *Claim Sheet* (page 91) • *My Claim* (page 92) • sentence strips, large index cards, or sheets of paper • chart paper • clothespins • scissors • bowl

Preparation Note: Prior to the lesson, make a response card for each student in the class by writing the following words around the perimeter of a sentence strip, a large index card, or a sheet of paper: *claim*, *counterclaim*, *reason*, and *evidence*. Laminate for durability, if desired.

Procedures

Model

1. Ask students whether they think that all schools should require students to wear uniforms. Record students' thoughts on a sheet of chart paper.

2. Distribute the *Making a Claim* activity sheet (page 90) to students. Discuss the terms *claim*, *counterclaim*, *reason*, and *evidence*. As a class, identify the claim and counterclaim from Step 1, and have students write these at the top of their activity sheets. Instruct students to independently write the ideas recorded on the chart paper into the appropriate box on their activity sheets.

3. Explain the *Response Cards* strategy to the class. (For detailed information on this strategy, see page 16.) Show students a response card, and model how to use it by reading a phrase from the chart paper and then placing the clothespin in the appropriate location.

4. Give each student a response card and a clothespin. Have students practice using the strategy by reading statements from the chart paper and asking other students to show their responses on their cards. When students disagree about a statement, stop and discuss the response.

Making a Claim *(cont.)*

Apply/Analyze

5. Assign each student a partner and distribute a *Claim Sheet* activity sheet (page 91) to each student pair. Provide students with a claim (e.g., video games should be considered art, people should be allowed to keep potentially dangerous animals as pets), and have them work together to write the counterclaim, reasons, and evidence.

6. Distribute scissors, and have students cut their *Claim Sheets* into strips along the designated lines. Collect all the strips, and place them in a bowl.

7. Randomly pick a strip from the bowl, and read it aloud. Have students identify the purpose of the statement, using the *Response Cards* strategy.

Evaluate/Create

8. Have students discuss their answers with their partners. Encourage them to explain why they chose their answers, even if they chose the same one as their partners.

9. Discuss the answers and students' reasoning as a class. Be sure to address differences in thinking.

10. Repeat Steps 7–9 as desired.

11. Distribute a *My Claim* activity sheet (page 92) to each student. Have students write paragraphs that include a claim, reasons, and evidence using the paragraph frames on the sheet.

12. Using the same partners from Step 8, assign one student the role of Partner *A* and the other the role of Partner *B*. Have Partner *A* read the entirety of his or her paragraph aloud to Partner *B*.

13. Have Partner *A* read one sentence from the paragraph aloud (not in order), and instruct Partner *B* to identify the purpose of the sentence, using his or her response card. Tell Partner *B* to explain his or her answer to Partner *A*, and then have Partner *A* reveal the correct answer, using his or her response card. Have partners discuss their thinking with each other. Repeat this process with the rest of the sentences from Partner *A*'s paragraph.

14. Switch roles and repeat Steps 12–13 until all of the sentences from the paragraphs have been read and identified.

Name: _____   Date: _____

Making a Claim

Directions: Write the claim and counterclaim in the top boxes. Fill in the reason(s) and the evidence in the boxes below.

Claim	Counterclaim
Reason	**Reason**
Evidence	**Evidence**

Name: _____ Date: _____

Claim Sheet

· ·

Directions: Write your assigned claim in the top box. Write a counterclaim in the second box. Develop reasons and evidence to support your claim and write them in the appropriate boxes. Then, cut apart the strips.

Claim

Counterclaim

Reason

Reason

Evidence

Evidence

Evidence

Name: _____   Date: _____

My Claim

· ·

Directions: Create your own persuasive paragraph, using the prompts below. Then, rewrite your complete paragraph on a separate sheet of paper.

Claim/Opening Sentence: I believe that _____

_____

_____

Reason(s): I think this because _____

_____

_____

Evidence/Examples

Point #1 _____

_____

Point #2 _____

_____

Point #3 _____

_____

Concluding Statement

_____

_____

_____

Lines and Planes: Mapping Rational Numbers

Brain-Powered Strategy	Standard
Response Cards	Find and position integers and other rational numbers on a horizontal or a vertical number-line diagram; find and position pairs of integers and other rational numbers on a coordinate plane

Vocabulary Words

- coordinate plane
- integer pairs
- number line
- rational numbers

Materials

- *Number Line and Coordinate Plane* (page 95)
- *Number Squares* (page 96)
- *Response Cards* (page 97)
- *My Integer Pairs and Answers* (page 98)
- small objects to use as markers (e.g., pennies, buttons)
- paper bags
- clothespins
- scissors

Preparation Note: Prior to the lesson, make a copy of *Number Squares* (page 96) and cut apart the cards. Place all of the cards in a bag. Additionally, make copies of the *Response Cards* (page 97) for each student. You may wish to precut and laminate the cards for durability.

Procedures

Model

1. Distribute the *Number Line and Coordinate Plane* activity sheet (page 95) to students. Give each student a small object to use as a marker.

2. As a review, go over the terms *rational number* and *number line* with students, and have them practice identifying numbers on a number line. Randomly select a number square from the bag, and read it aloud. Have students place their markers on the number line in the appropriate place.

3. Remind students how coordinate planes work. Have them identify the *x*–axis and *y*–axis. Go over the different quadrants and their labels.

Lines and Planes: Mapping Rational Numbers *(cont.)*

4. Explain the *Response Cards* strategy to the class. (For detailed information on this strategy, see page 16.) Model the strategy by selecting two numbers from the bag, writing the integer pair on the board, placing the marker in the correct location on the coordinate plane on the *Number Line and Coordinate Plane* activity sheet, and then using the clothespin to identify the correct quadrant on the *Response Cards* activity sheet (page 97).

5. Distribute a *Response Card* and a clothespin to each student. Draw two different numbers from the bag, and write the integer pair on the board. Have students practice placing their markers on the activity sheets and then using their *Response Cards* to indicate the correct quadrant for the pair of integers.

Apply/Analyze

6. Assign each student a partner, and distribute a *Number Squares* activity sheet and a paper bag to each student pair. Have students cut the number squares apart and place them in the bags.

7. Instruct students to take turns pulling two numbers from bags to make integer pairs. Working independently, have both students use their markers to show the locations of the pairs on the coordinate planes. Then, have students indicate the quadrants of the integer pairs, using their *Response Cards.* Tell students to hold up their cards at the same time and compare answers.

Evaluate/Create

8. Tell students to discuss their answers with their partners. Even if the two partners chose the same answer, they should still explain their reasoning and discuss their thinking aloud.

9. Repeat Steps 7–8 as desired.

10. Distribute a *My Integer Pairs and Answers* activity sheet (page 98) to each student. Have students write their own integer pairs, related questions, and answers in the answer key.

11. Using the same partners from Step 6, have each student take a turn reading a question or integer pair from his or her activity sheet to his or her partner. The other partner uses his or her *Response Card* to indicate the answer and then explains why he or she chose that particular answer. Finally, the first partner reveals the correct answer, using his or her *Response Card,* and the two partners discuss their thinking with each other.

12. Instruct partners to continue switching roles and repeating Steps 10–11 as time allows.

Name: _____ Date: _____

Number Line and Coordinate Plane

Directions: Use your marker to indicate where the rational numbers belong on either the number line or the coordinate plane.

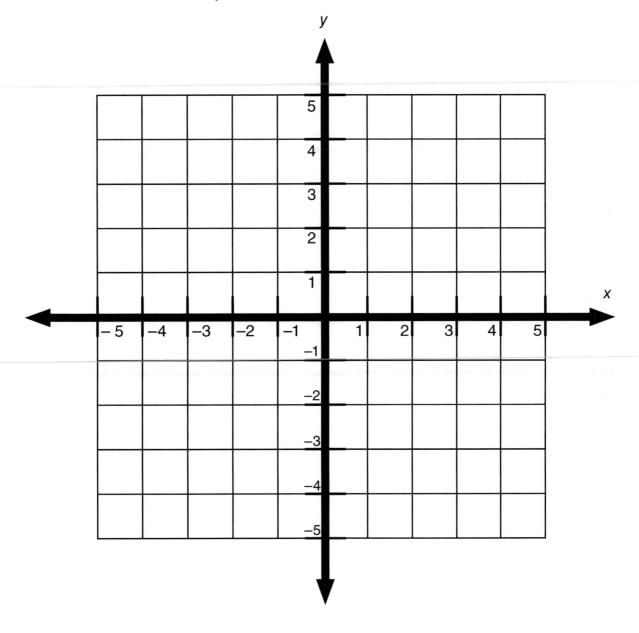

Number Squares

Directions: Cut apart the number squares and place them in a paper bag.

0	0	4	4	−3	−3
1	1	5	5	−4	−4
2	2	−1	−1	−5	−5
3	3	−2	−2	0	0

#51183—*Brain-Powered Lessons to Engage All Learners* © *Shell Education*

Response Cards

Directions: Cut out the card below. Clip your clothespin onto the card in the correct quadrant to indicate your answer.

Quadrant II

Quadrant I

Quadrant III

Quadrant IV

Name: _____ Date: _____

My Integer Pairs and Answers

Directions: Write four integer pairs on the lines below. Then, write questions that use the same answers as shown on your response card. Use the bottom of the activity sheet to create an answer key.

My Integer Pairs

1. _____

2. _____

3. _____

4. _____

My Questions

1. _____

2. _____

3. _____

4. _____

My Answer Key

1. _____

2. _____

3. _____

4. _____

Word Detective

Brain-Powered Strategy	**Standard**
Response Cards	Use common, grade-appropriate Greek or Latin affixes and roots as clues to the meaning of a word

Vocabulary Words	**Materials**
• affix	• *Drawing Meaning from Affixes* (page 101)
• etymology	• *Word Tree Diagram* (page 102)
• prefix	• *Word Diagrams* (page 103)
• root word	• *My Questions and Answers* (page 104)
• suffix	• sentence strips, large index cards, or sheets of paper
	• clothespins
	• dictionaries, thesauri, and other resources

Preparation Note: Prior to the lesson, make one response card for each student in the class by writing the following words around the perimeter of a sentence strip, a large index card, or a sheet of paper: *prefix*, *suffix*, and *root word*. Laminate for durability, if desired.

Procedures

Model

1. Review the terms *etymology, prefix, suffix,* and *root word* with students. Assign each student a partner, and distribute a *Drawing Meaning from Affixes* activity sheet (page 101) to each student pair. Instruct students to work together to complete the activity sheet.

2. Discuss the meanings of the root words and affixes from the *Drawing Meaning from Affixes* activity sheet as a class.

prefix *ex-* without, not including	**suffix** *-est* most
prefix *mis-* lack of, wrong	**suffix** *-less* without
prefix *in-* into, toward	**suffix** *-ologist* one who studies a particular kind of science

Word Detective *(cont.)*

3. Display the *Word Tree Diagram* activity sheet (page 102) on the board or projector. As a class, work together to diagram the word *predominates.*

4. Explain the *Response Cards* strategy to students. (For detailed information on this strategy, see page 16.) Show them a response card, and demonstrate how to use the card by asking the question *In the word biography, -graph is the _____ that means "to write."* Clip the clothespin to *root word* and explain your thinking aloud.

Apply/Analyze

5. Give each pair of students a *Word Diagrams* activity sheet (page 103), and write the following four words on the board: *contribution, revolutionary, preceded,* and *undivided.* Have students work together to diagram two of the words using dictionaries, thesauri, and other resources with information on the etymology of words.

6. When students have completed their activity sheets, ask them to respond to your questions by holding up their response cards at the same time. Some sample questions might include:

- In the word *undivided*, the *-ed* part of the word is the _____.

- The *-vol* portion of the word *revolutionary* is the _____.

- *Con-* means "with" or "together." What part does it play in the word *contribution*?

Evaluate/Create

7. Encourage students to share the reasoning behind their answers with their classmates. Discuss any differences in thinking and review the word diagrams as a class.

8. Distribute a *My Questions and Answers* activity sheet (page 104) to each student. Have students independently write their own questions that have the same answers as are shown on their response cards.

9. Using the same partners from Step 1, assign one student the role of Partner *A* and the other student the role of Partner *B*. To start, have Partner *A* ask a question from his or her activity sheet to Partner *B*. Partner *B* responds by showing the answer on his or her response card. The responding partner should also give an explanation of why he or she made that choice.

10. After Partner *B* responds and explains his or her response, Partner *A* then uses his or her response card to reveal the correct answer. After both partners have given answers, ask them to discuss their thinking with each other.

11. Switch roles and repeat Steps 9–10 until all of the questions have been asked and answered or as time allows.

Name: _____ Date: _____

Drawing Meaning from Affixes

Directions: Look at the groups of words below that share the same affix. Think about the meanings of the words and any similarities among them. Write what you think the affix means.

prefix *ex-*

exterior

external

exclude

Meaning: _____

_____

prefix *mis-*

mistreat

misplace

misfortune

Meaning: _____

_____

prefix *in-*

inactive

incomplete

incorrect

Meaning: _____

_____

suffix *-est*

strongest

fastest

longest

Meaning: _____

_____

suffix *-less*

humorless

effortless

careless

Meaning: _____

_____

suffix *-ologist*

biologist

dermatologist

pharmacologist

Meaning: _____

_____

Word Tree Diagram

Directions: Write the target word at the top of the tree. Write the prefix, root word, and/or suffix at the base of the tree. Then, write other words that share the same root on the leaves.

Target Word

Prefix   **Root Word**   **Suffix**

Name: _____   Date: _____

Word Diagrams

Directions: Write the target word at the top of the tree. Write the prefix, root word, and/or suffix at the base of the tree. Then, write other words that share the same root on the leaves.

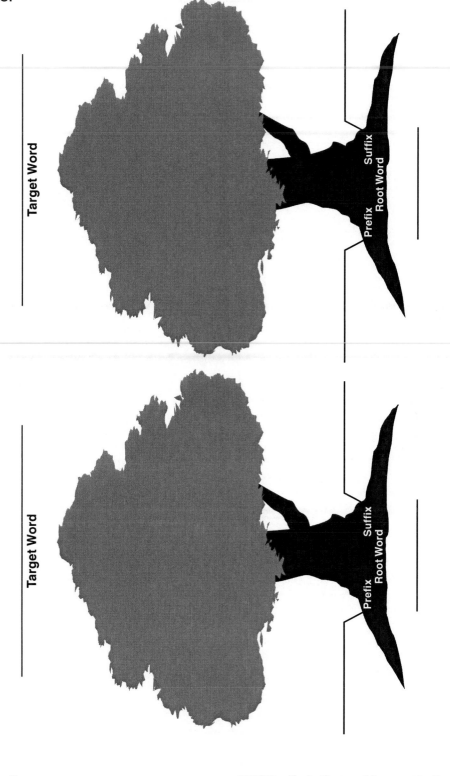

Name: _____ Date: _____

My Questions and Answers

Directions: Write at least five questions that have the same answers as shown on your response card. Use the bottom of the activity sheet to create the answer key.

My Questions

1. _____

2. _____

3. _____

4. _____

5. _____

My Answer Key

1. _____

2. _____

3. _____

4. _____

5. _____

Revolutionary War Leaders

Brain-Powered Strategy
Matchmaker

Standard
Understands the major developments and chronology of the Revolutionary War and the roles of its political, military, and diplomatic leaders

Vocabulary Words

- John Adams
- Samuel Adams
- Benjamin Franklin
- Thomas Jefferson
- George Washington

Materials

- *Revolutionary War Leaders Cards* (page 107)
- *Revolutionary War Biography* (page 108)
- address labels
- research materials (e.g., textbooks, Internet resources, articles)
- index cards

Preparation Note: Prior to the lesson, write the vocabulary words on address labels. Make enough labels so that each student will have one label to wear. Copy and cut out five sets of the *Revolutionary War Leaders Cards* (page 107).

Procedures

Model

1. Divide the class into five groups, and assign each group a name from the vocabulary words listed above. Have students in each group research their assigned leader, using their textbooks, the Internet, and other relevant resources.

2. Have students work together to create a list of the five most important facts about their assigned person. Distribute five index cards to each student. Instruct students to list people's names on the front sides of the index cards and five chosen facts on the backs.

3. Assign each student in the group a number 1–5 (if there are more than five students per group, give some students the same number). Create new groups by asking all the number ones to sit together, all the number twos to sit together, and so on. Give each student three minutes to present his or her five facts to the rest of the group. While one group member is presenting, the other group members should take notes on their remaining index cards. At the end of the 15 minutes, all students should have completed their index cards with five facts for each individual.

Revolutionary War Leaders *(cont.)*

Apply/Analyze

4. Tell students to remain in their groups of five. Give each student an address label with one name on it to wear. Have students stand in a circle, and put a set of *Revolutionary War Leaders Cards* on the floor in the middle of the circle. You may wish to use the enlarged versions of these cards found on the Digital Resource CD (filename: warleaderscards.pdf).

5. Explain the instructions for the *Matchmaker* strategy, and guide them through the playing of the first round. (For detailed information on this strategy, see page 17.)

6. After completing the first round, have students mix up the cards and return them to the center of the circle. Give them time to play again, and instruct students to make sure they pick up a different card from last time.

Evaluate/Create

7. Distribute a *Revolutionary War Biography* activity sheet (page 108) to students. Have students choose one of the five figures they have been studying and complete the activity sheet. In their biographies, students should include the five facts from their *Revolutionary War Leaders Notes* (Step 3) and also include additional information about the person.

8. Allow students time to share their *Revolutionary War Biography* activity sheets with a peer and/or the rest of the class.

9. If time permits, have students research and complete additional *Revolutionary War Biographies* for other leaders, such as John Hancock and Richard Henry Lee.

Revolutionary War Leaders Cards

Teacher Directions: Copy and cut apart five sets of the cards below. Give one set to each group of five students.

◎ I served as commander in chief of the Continental (American) Army during the Revolutionary War.

◎ I was elected president of the convention that wrote the United States Constitution.

◎ I served two terms as the first president of the United States.

◎ My picture is on the one-dollar bill.

◎ I served on the Second Continental Congress and helped draft the Declaration of Independence.

◎ I helped negotiate the Treaty of Paris in 1783 that ended the Revolutionary War.

◎ As ambassador to France, I persuaded the French to give large amounts of money, supplies, and manpower to aid the American effort to defeat the British.

◎ I was a delegate to the convention that wrote the United States Constitution.

◎ I was elected to write the Declaration of Independence by the Second Continental Congress.

◎ I served as governor of Virginia.

◎ My family and I were nearly captured by British troops in Virginia.

◎ I served as vice president under John Adams and later became the third president of the United States.

◎ I helped persuade Congress to choose George Washington to lead the Continental Army.

◎ My letters to and from my wife, Abigail, are important artifacts from this period in history.

◎ I was the first vice president of the United States and the second president of the United States.

◎ My son became the sixth president of the United States.

◎ I was a delegate to the Continental Congress and signed the Declaration of Independence.

◎ I worked with John Hancock to form the Sons of Liberty, a coalition of colonial activists.

◎ I helped incite the protests that eventually led to the Boston Massacre in 1770 and the Boston Tea Party in 1773.

◎ I helped draft the Articles of Confederation and the Massachusetts Constitution.

Name: _____ Date: _____

Revolutionary War Biography

Directions: Choose a leader from the Revolutionary War period and draw his or her picture in the box below. Then, write a short biography of this person on the lines at the bottom of the page.

_____

_____

_____

_____

_____

Equivalent Expressions

Brain-Powered Strategy	**Standard**
Matchmaker	Apply the properties of operations to generate equivalent expressions

Vocabulary Words

- associative property
- commutative property
- distributive property
- equivalent expressions
- properties of operations

Materials

- *Find My Match Cards* (pages 111–112)
- *Equivalent Expressions* (page 113)
- *Math Expression Cards* (page 114)
- *Math Expressions A* (page 115)
- *Math Expressions B* (page 115)
- address labels
- bowl
- index cards

Preparation Note: Prior to the lesson, prepare the address labels by writing one of the following expressions on each label: *2x + 1, 3y, 4(a + b), a + 5 + b, 3(10)*. Make enough sets so that each student will have one address label. In addition, cut apart the *Math Expression Cards* (page 114) and the *Find My Match Cards* (pages 111–112).

Procedures

Model

1. Review the *properties of operations* with the class. Demonstrate how to make *equivalent expressions* using the *associative*, *commutative*, and *distributive* properties.

2. Put all of the *Find My Match Cards* in a bowl, and have each student draw a card. Instruct students to walk around the classroom and find other students with cards with equivalent expressions.

3. After students have sorted themselves into groups with equivalent expressions, have them return to their seats, and distribute the *Equivalent Expressions* activity sheet (page 113) to students. Have students work independently to complete the activity sheet and then discuss the answers as a class.

Equivalent Expressions *(cont.)*

Apply/Analyze

4. Explain the instructions for the *Matchmaker* strategy to students. (For detailed information on this strategy, see page 17.)

5. Divide students into groups of five, and distribute address labels with numerical expressions on them to each student. Place a set of *Math Expression Cards* in the center of the group. You may wish to use the enlarged versions of these cards found on the Digital Resource CD (filename: mathexpressioncards.pdf). Guide students through the playing of the first round.

6. After completing the first round, have students mix up the cards, and return them to the center of the circle. Give them time to play again, and instruct students to make sure they pick up different cards than the last time.

Evaluate/Create

7. Distribute either a *Math Expressions A* activity sheet (page 115) or a *Math Expressions B* activity sheet (page 115) to each student. Have them complete the sheets independently.

8. Distribute four index cards to each student, and have them cut the cards in half so that they have a total of eight cards. Instruct students to write the four printed expressions that were already on the sheet and the four equivalent expressions they developed on the cards, one expression per card.

9. Place students in groups of three, and have them put all of their cards facedown in the middle of the group. Mix up the cards, and then arrange them in a 6 × 4 grid. Have students take turns trying to find matches of equivalent expressions. When it is a student's turn, he or she turns over two cards. If the cards show equivalent expressions, the student removes the match from the game and keeps it. If the expressions are not equivalent, the students turns them back over. When all of the cards have been matched, the player with the most matches wins.

Find My Match Cards

Teacher Directions: Cut apart the cards below, and place them in a bag or a bowl.

$(a + b) + (c + d)$	$(a + c) + (b + d)$	$a + b + c + d$
$(d + a) + (b + c)$	$4a$	$a + a + a + a$
$2a + 2a$	$a + 3a$	$3 \times b \times a$
$a \times 3 \times b$	$a \times b \times 3$	$3ab$
$3(2 + 4n)$	$6 + 12n$	$2(3 + 6n)$

Find My Match Cards *(cont.)*

$x(4 + 1)$	$4x + x$	$5x$
$4a(2 + 3)$	$8a + 12a$	$20a$
$(4a)(5)$	$2a(4 + 6)$	$(2a)(10)$
$6(3a + 3)$	$18a + 18$	$18(a + 1)$
$2(a + 1 + 3)$	$2a + 2 + 6$	$2a + 8$

   #51183—*Brain-Powered Lessons to Engage All Learners*

Name: _____   Date: _____

Equivalent Expressions

Directions: On the lines below each expression, write equivalent expressions.

1. $(a + b) + (c + d)$

_____

_____

_____

_____

2. $4a$

_____

_____

_____

3. $3 \times b \times a$

_____

_____

_____

4. $3(2 + 4n)$

_____

_____

_____

_____

5. $x(4 + 1)$

_____

_____

_____

6. $4a(2 + 3)$

_____

_____

_____

Math Expression Cards

Teacher Directions: Copy and cut apart the cards below. Make enough sets so there is a set for each group of five students.

$x + x + 1$	$y + y + y$
$4a + 4b$	$5 + b + a$
$3(3 + 7)$	

Name: _____   Date: _____

Math Expressions A

....

Directions: Below each math expression, write one equivalent expression.

1. $a + 2 + 3$ _____	**3.** $5a(2 + 3)$ _____
2. $3(y + 1)$ _____	**4.** $y + y + y + y$ _____

- -

Name: _____   Date: _____

Math Expressions B

....

Directions: Below each math expression, write one equivalent expression.

1. $2(a + 4)$ _____	**3.** $2n(2 + 4)$ _____
2. $y + 0 + 3$ _____	**4.** $6y$ _____

Investigating Inferences

Brain-Powered Strategy	Standard
Matchmaker	Cite textual evidence to support analysis of what the text says explicitly as well as inferences drawn from the text

Vocabulary Words

- explicit reference
- inference
- textual evidence

Materials

- *Inferences and Text References* (page 118)
- *Inference Cards* (page 119)
- *Feedback Notes* (page 120)
- address labels
- reading passage appropriate for making inferences

Preparation Note: Prior to the lesson, prepare the address labels by writing one of the following sentences on each label. Prepare enough sets of labels so that each student will have one. Additionally, copy and cut apart the *Inference Cards* (page 119). Make enough copies so that each student receives one card.

- I recently had a falling out with a close friend.
- Sam is scared of dogs.
- I am in a desert.
- I am very cold.
- It is the morning and I need to get up, but I'm too tired.

Procedures

Model

1. Review the concept of inferences with students. Write the sample sentence *My heart pounded, and my palms began to sweat as I stared out at the crowded auditorium.* Ask students what they can infer from the sentence. Record their ideas on the board.

2. Explain the importance of using explicit text references when providing support for an inference. Distribute a reading passage to students, and ask them to read the selection independently.

Investigating Inferences (cont.)

3. Assign each student a partner. Distribute the *Inferences and Text References* activity sheet (page 118) to each student pair. Have students work together to draw inferences from the reading, and support their inferences with explicit text references.

Apply/Analyze

4. Explain the instructions for the *Matchmaker* strategy to students. (For detailed information on this strategy, see page 17.)

5. Divide students into groups of five, and give each student an address label to wear. Place a set of *Inference Cards* (page 119) in the center of the group. You may wish to use the enlarged versions of these cards found on the Digital Resource CD (filename: inferencecards.pdf). Guide students through the playing of the first round.

6. When students have finished the first round, have them mix up the cards and return them to the center of the circle. Give the groups time to play again, and tell students to make sure they pick up different cards from the last time.

Evaluate/Create

7. Have students write their own paragraphs that require the reader to make inferences on a topic of their choosing.

8. Instruct students to switch paragraphs with a partner, and read their partner's writing. Distribute the *Feedback Notes* activity sheet (page 120) to students. Tell students to record the inferences that he or she was able to make from the paragraph on the *Feedback Notes* activity sheet. They also should record any suggestions they have on how to improve the paragraph.

9. Ask the partners to come back together and give their partners the *Feedback Notes* activity sheets. Instruct students to share the inferences they made from their partner's writing sample and any questions or suggestions they have to help improve the paragraph.

10. Allow students to revise their paragraphs to incorporate the feedback from their partners. On the final version of the paragraph, have students list the inference(s) they hope the reader derives from their writing underneath the paragraph.

ferences and Text References

Directions: Record the inferences you were able to make from the passage. Underneath the inference statement, write the text from which you made the inference.

1. **Inference:** _____

   _____

   Text Reference: _____

   _____

   _____

2. **Inference:** _____

   _____

   Text Reference: _____

   _____

   _____

3. **Inference:** _____

   _____

   Text Reference: _____

   _____

   _____

4. **Inference:** _____

   _____

   Text Reference: _____

   _____

   _____

Inference Cards

Teacher Directions: Copy and cut apart the cards below. Make enough sets so there is a set for each group of five students.

I felt my body grow tense when she entered the room. She avoided making eye contact with me and immediately went to sit with the other girls. I tried not to think about how close we once were, but it was no good—all the memories came flooding back.

The moment Sam saw the dog, he started to shake and immediately forgot what he was saying to me.

The sun beat down mercilessly, and the ground burned under my feet. Sand dunes stretched off into the distance in every direction.

My teeth chattered, and I pulled my hood so tight that only my eyes were visible.

My eyelids felt like they were made out of lead. I attempted to pry them open, but they quickly slammed shut again. My alarm clock continued to beep incessantly as the early morning sunlight streamed through a crack in my blinds.

Name: _____ Date: _____

Feedback Notes

Directions: Record the inferences that you were able to make while reading your partner's paragraph. At the bottom, write any questions or suggestions you have to help your partner improve his or her paragraph.

Inferences

_____

_____

_____

_____

_____

_____

_____

Feedback/Suggestions/Questions

_____

_____

_____

_____

_____

_____

Perfect Paragraphs

Brain-Powered Strategy	**Standard**
Just Say It	Develop the topic with relevant facts, definitions, concrete details, quotations, or other information and examples

Vocabulary Words

- concrete details
- definitions
- quotations
- relevant facts

Materials

- *Topic Development* (page 123)
- *Just Say It Notes* (page 124)
- *Paragraph Design* (page 125)
- timer
- research materials (e.g., textbooks, Internet, journal articles)

Procedures

Model

1. Review the terms *relevant facts, definitions, concrete details*, and *quotations* with the class. Emphasize how these components can be used to develop a topic when writing a paragraph or an essay.

2. Distribute the *Topic Development* activity sheet (page 123) to students. Write a recent topic of study (e.g., factors that affect Earth's climate) on the board, and ask students to share their background knowledge on the subject. Record their ideas on the board, and have students record them on their activity sheets.

3. Give students time to do additional research on the topic. Encourage them to look in books and on the Internet to find more details and supporting quotations to add to their activity sheets.

4. Using their notes, ask each student to write a paragraph on the topic of study at the bottom of their activity sheet.

Perfect Paragraphs *(cont.)*

Apply/Analyze

5. Assign each student a partner, and have the pairs sit facing each other at their desks. Ask partners to switch *Topic Development* activity sheets and read each other's paragraphs.

6. Explain the *Just Say It* strategy to the class. (For detailed information on this strategy, see page 18.) Distribute the *Just Say It Notes* activity sheet (page 124) to students. Help students identify themselves as either Partner *A* or Partner *B*. Set a timer for 30 seconds, and ask all of the Partner *A*s in the class to share their thoughts about their partner's paragraph while all of the Partner *B*s listen. All Partner *B*s should take notes on the feedback on their *Just Say It Notes* activity sheet. Then, provide time for the Partner *B*s to respond. Switch roles, and repeat the exercise.

7. Once both partners have had chances to talk and give feedback, instruct students to review their notes from the *Just Say It Notes* activity sheet and then revise their paragraphs to incorporate their partners' feedback.

Evaluate/Create

8. Distribute a *Paragraph Design* activity sheet (page 125) to each student. Give students time to research topics of their choosing and complete the necessary information on the activity sheets.

9. Using their notes, have students write paragraphs about the new topics on the bottom of their activity sheets.

10. Repeat the *Just Say It* strategy using the new student-written paragraphs and new *Just Say It Notes* activity sheets.

11. When both students have shared their paragraphs and received feedback from their partners, give students time to revise their paragraphs and incorporate the feedback.

Name: _____   Date: _____

Topic Development

Directions: Write the notes from the class in the top box. Record additional notes from your research in the middle box. Then, use the information from your notes to write a paragraph on the topic of study.

Topic: _____

Class Notes
Additional Research Notes
Paragraph

Name: _____ Date: _____

Just Say It Notes

Directions: Record the feedback your partner gives you in the space below. Then at the bottom of the page, write how you can use this feedback to improve your writing.

Notes on Feedback

_____

_____

_____

_____

_____

Plans to Incorporate the Feedback

_____

_____

_____

_____

_____

_____

Name: _____ Date: _____

Paragraph Design

Directions: Write your topic on the line below. Record the details you plan to use to develop your topic in the appropriate boxes. Then, write your paragraph on the lines below.

Topic: _____

Facts	Definitions	Quotations
Other		

Paragraph

_____

_____

_____

_____

_____

Rad Ratios

Brain-Powered Strategy	Standard
Just Say It	Understand the concept of a ratio and use ratio language to describe a ratio relationship between two quantities

Vocabulary Words

- percentage
- proportion
- ratio

Materials

- *Ratio Cards* (pages 128–130)
- *Understanding Ratios* (page 131)
- *Ratio Word Problem* (page 132)
- *Just Say It Word Problem* (page 133)
- *Just Say It Notes* (page 124)
- *My Ratio* (page 134)
- timer

Preparation Note: Prior to the lesson, cut apart the *Ratio Cards* (pages 128–130).

Procedures

Model

1. Distribute one *Ratio Card* to each student. You may wish to use the enlarged versions of these cards found on the Digital Resource CD (filename: ratiocards.pdf).Half of the students will have a picture on their card, and the other half will have a number ratio. Instruct students to walk around the classroom and find students with matching cards so that each pair of students has one picture and one number ratio that represent the same relationship.

2. Distribute the *Understanding Ratios* activity sheet (page 131) to students. When all students have found a match, have them record both the picture and the number ratio from the cards on their activity sheets.

3. Review the terms *ratio*, *proportion*, and *percentage* with the class. Provide examples of how to change a ratio to a percentage. Have students convert the number ratios to percentages on their *Understanding Ratios* activity sheets.

4. Display the *Ratio Word Problem* (page 132) on the board or projector. Ask students how they would go about finding the answer to the problem. Think aloud as you work through the problem, and write down the answer.

5. Instruct students to work together with their partners to brainstorm word problems to represent their ratio on their *Understanding Ratios* activity sheets.

Rad Ratios *(cont.)*

Apply/Analyze

6. Assign students a new partner, and have the partners sit at desks facing each other. Explain the *Just Say It* strategy to the class. (For detailed information on this strategy, see page 18.)

7. Help students identify themselves as either Partner *A* or Partner *B*. Distribute the *Just Say It Word Problem* activity sheet (page 133) and *Just Say It Notes* activity sheet (page 124) to students, and ask them to read the word problem. Set a timer for 30 seconds, and ask all of the Partner *A*s in the class to share their thoughts and knowledge about the word problem while all of the Partner *B*s listen. Then, provide time for the Partner *B*s to respond. All Partner *A*s should take notes on their partner's feedback, using the *Just Say It Notes* activity sheet. Switch roles, and repeat the exercise.

8. Once both partners have had chances to talk and give feedback, instruct students to review their notes from the *Just Say It Notes* activity sheet and then solve the problem on the bottom of their activity sheet.

9. Review the problem and solution with the class.

Evaluate/Create

10. Distribute a *My Ratio* activity sheet (page 134) to each student. Have students work together with their partners to complete the activity sheet by creating ratios, drawings, percentages, and word problems.

11. Assign new partners, and repeat the *Just Say It* strategy, using the ratios and word problems created on the *My Ratio* activity sheets.

12. When both students have shared their work and received feedback from their partners, give students time to revise their activity sheets and incorporate the feedback.

Ratio Cards

Teacher Directions: Cut apart the cards below. Distribute one to each student.

3:1		**3:8**	
1:2		**5:8**	
1:4		**3:10**	

Ratio Cards *(cont.)*

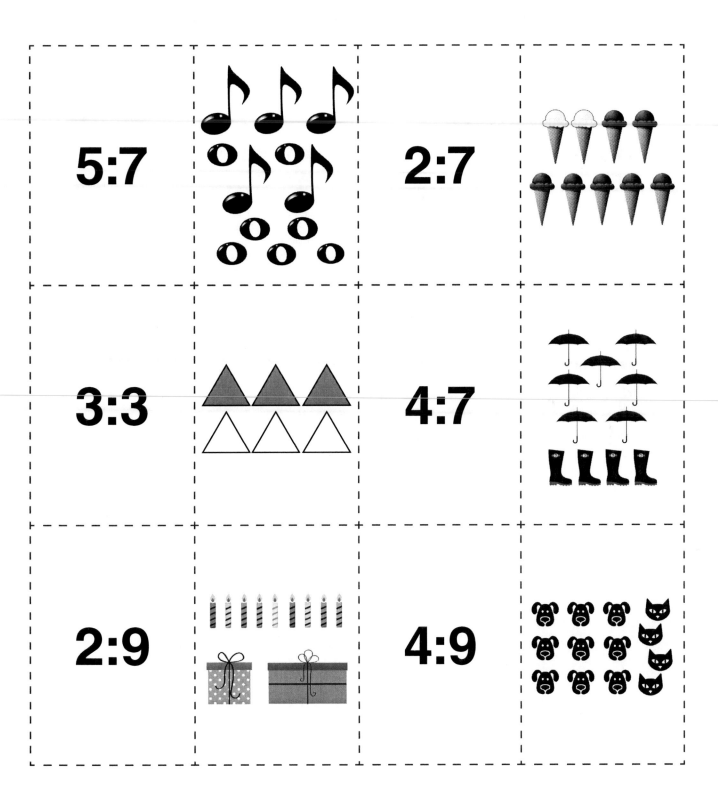

Ratio Cards *(cont.)*

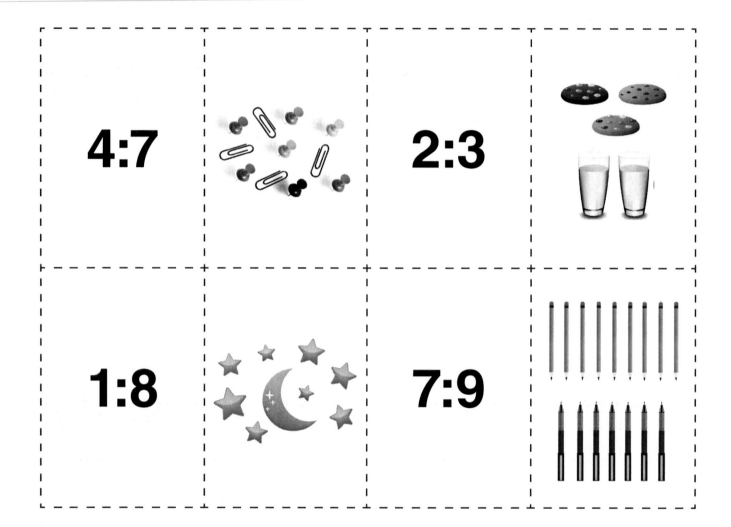

#51183—Brain-Powered Lessons to Engage All Learners   © Shell Education

Name: _____   Date: _____

Understanding Ratios

· ·

Directions: Record the ratio and matching picture from you and your partner's cards in the space below. When instructed to by your teacher, write the corresponding percentage and create a word problem to go with your ratio.

Ratio	Picture	Percentage

Word Problem
_____
_____
_____
_____
_____
_____
_____

Ratio Word Problem

The sixth graders in Ms. Smith's class had an ice cream social on Friday. Every student had a choice of chocolate or vanilla ice cream. Thirteen students chose vanilla ice cream, and 16 students chose chocolate ice cream. What is the ratio of students who chose chocolate ice cream to the number of students who chose vanilla ice cream?

Name: _____ Date: _____

Just Say It Word Problem

Directions: Read the word problem below. Complete the *Just Say It* strategy with your partner. Then, answer the problem.

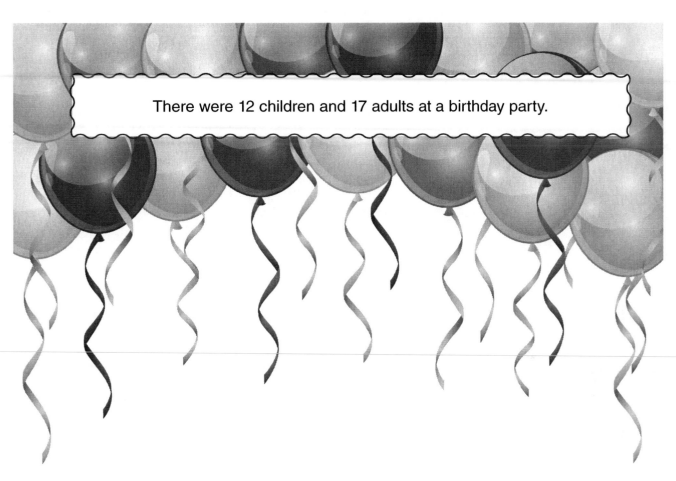

There were 12 children and 17 adults at a birthday party.

1. What was the ratio of adults to children at the party?

    _____

2. What was the ratio of children to total people at the party?

    _____

3. Three more children came to the party. What is the ratio of adults to total people at the party now?

    _____

Name: _____   Date: _____

My Ratio

Directions: Working together with your partner, choose a ratio and write it in the first box. Record the corresponding percentage. Create an illustration and a word problem to go with your ratio.

Ratio	Percentage	Illustration

Word Problem

Energy: A Case of Multiple Identities

Brain-Powered Strategy	**Standard**
Just Say It	Knows that energy is a property of many substances

Vocabulary Words

- chemical energy
- electrical energy
- mechanical energy
- thermal energy

Materials

- *Energy Cards* (page 137)
- *Energy Picture* (page 138)
- *Just Say It Notes* (page 124)
- *My Energy Picture* (page 139)
- research materials (e.g., textbooks, Internet)
- index cards
- timer

Preparation Note: Prior to the lesson, cut apart the *Energy Cards* (page 137).

Procedures

Model

1. Divide the class into four groups, and distribute an *Energy Card* to each group. Ask students in each group to research the type of energy shown on their card, using their textbooks, the Internet, and other print or electronic resources. Distribute four index cards to students, and have them record the information they learned on one card.

2. Ask one representative from each group to come to the front of the class and share their group's information about their *Energy Card*. All other students should record notes on their remaining index cards.

3. Explain that this lesson focuses on four major types of energy: *thermal, chemical, mechanical,* and *electrical.* Remind students that there are other types of energy, such as nuclear and electromagnetic energy, that they will learn about at a later time.

4. Review the four types of energy on the *Energy Cards.* Highlight the main features of each type of energy, and discuss how each group's picture relates to a specific type of energy.

Energy: A Case of Multiple Identities *(cont.)*

Apply/Analyze

5. Assign each student a partner, and have the partners sit at their desks facing each other. Explain the *Just Say It* strategy to the class. (For detailed information on this strategy, see page 18.) Distribute an *Energy Picture* activity sheet (page 138) to each student pair.

6. Help students identify themselves as either Partner *A* or Partner *B*. Set a timer for 30 seconds, and ask all of the Partner *A*s in the class to share their thoughts and knowledge about the image in the *Energy Picture* while all of the Partner *B*s listen. Then, provide time for the Partner *B*s to respond. All Partner *A*s should take notes on their partner's feedback, using the *Just Say It Notes* activity sheet. Switch roles, and repeat the exercise.

7. Once both partners have had chances to discuss and give feedback, instruct students to review their notes from their *Just Say It Notes* activity sheet. Have each student independently write a paragraph describing the type of energy shown in the picture.

8. Give students time to share and discuss their paragraphs with their partners.

Evaluate/Create

9. Tell students that they will create their own pictures to represent one of the four types of energy they have been studying in the lesson. Distribute the *My Energy Picture* activity sheet (page 139) to students, and have them write their chosen type of energy at the top of the sheet. Then, have them complete the rest of their activity sheet independently.

10. Assign new partners, and repeat the *Just Say It* strategy, using the student-created pictures and explanations.

11. When both students have shared their work and received feedback from their partners, give students time to revise their drawings and add additional details in order to incorporate the feedback.

Energy Cards

Teacher Directions: Cut apart the cards below. Distribute one to each group.

Name: _____   Date: _____

Energy Picture

. . . .

Directions: Examine the picture below. What type of energy is represented in the picture? What makes you think so?

Name: _____ Date: _____

My Energy Picture

Directions: Write the type of energy on the top line. Draw a picture showing an example of this type of energy. Write an explanation of the picture in the space at the bottom of the page.

Type of energy: _____

Picture

Explanation

_____

_____

_____

_____

_____

Women and War

Brain-Powered Strategy	Standard
Reverse, Reverse!	Understands the development of the post-World War II women's movement

Vocabulary Words

- gender equality
- women's movement

Materials

- *Before, During, and After* (page 142)
- *Paragraph Feedback* (page 143)
- research materials (e.g., textbooks, articles, electronic resources)
- index cards
- writing paper

Procedures

Model

1. Divide the class into groups of four. Distribute the *Before, During, and After* activity sheet (page 142) to students, and assign each student in the group one of the following topics:

   - United States economy
   - Jobs available to women
   - Female attitudes toward women in the workforce
   - Male attitudes toward women in the workforce

2. Using research materials or the Internet, have students research and record notes on the status of their topic before, during, and after World War II.

3. Ask students to go around the group and take turns sharing the information they learned about their topics. The other students in the group should take notes on the topics on their *Before, During, and After* activity sheets.

4. As a class, review each topic and highlight how the topics changed over the course of World War II. Encourage students to add to their notes on the activity sheets.

5. Distribute six index cards to each student. Discuss the following questions, and have students take notes about the causes and effects on their index cards:

   - How did changes in the United States economy affect male and female attitudes toward women in the workforce?

   - How did changes in the United States economy affect the jobs available to women?

   - How were male and female attitudes toward women in the workforce the same or different before, during, and after World War II?

Women and War *(cont.)*

Apply/Analyze

6. Have students sit or stand in a circle. Explain how to play the *Reverse, Reverse!* strategy. (For detailed information on this strategy, see page 19.)

7. Choose a student to be the judge, and have him or her sit outside the circle. Instruct the judge to halt the game if, at any point, students describe an event that does not relate to the event stated before.

8. Guide students in the playing of the first round of the game. Have the first student begin by stating a cause. The following students will state effects of the cause. Allow students to continue playing the game until the predetermined amount of time has passed.

11. Have students read the feedback from their partners and revise their paragraphs as they see fit.

12. Display the paragraphs on a classroom bulletin board. You may also choose to have students use these paragraphs as starting points for longer essays on the roles of women in the workforce before, during, and after World War II.

Evaluate/Create

9. After students finish playing *Reverse, Reverse!*, have them go back to their desks. Distribute writing paper to students, and ask each student to choose two of the four topics from Step 1, and write a paragraph examining how changes in one topic affected changes in the other topic (e.g., How did changes in the United States economy affect changes in the jobs available to women?).

10. Distribute the *Paragraph Feedback* activity sheet (page 143) to students. Assign each student a partner, and have the pairs read each other's paragraphs and provide feedback on their *Paragraph Feedback* activity sheets.

Name: _____ Date: _____

Before, During, and After

··

Directions: Write your assigned topic on the line below. Research your topic, and record notes in the appropriate boxes below.

Topic: _____

After World War II	
During World War II	
Before World War II	

Name: _____   Date: _____

Paragraph Feedback

Directions: Read your partner's paragraph. Provide feedback using the prompts below.

Topic #1:

Topic #2:

1. Did the paragraph describe how the two topics are connected? Why, or why not?

2. What could your partner do to improve his or her paragraph?

3. What did you like best about your partner's paragraph?

Equivalent Numbers:
One Quantity, Many Forms

Brain-Powered Strategy	Standard
Reverse, Reverse!	Understands the relationships among equivalent number representations

Vocabulary Words

- decimals
- equivalent numbers
- fractions
- improper fractions
- percentages

Materials

- *Equivalent Number Cards* (pages 146–147)
- *Equivalent Numbers* (page 148)
- *Converting Numbers* (page 149)
- *Number Application Cards* (pages 150–151)
- *My Word Problem* (page 152)
- bag or bowl
- blank sheets of paper

Prepartation Note: Prior to the lesson, cut apart the *Equivalent Number Cards* activity sheet (pages 146–147) and the *Number Application Cards* activity sheet (pages 150–151).

Procedures

Model

1. Distribute one *Equivalent Number Card* to each student. You may wish to use the enlarged versions of these cards found on the Digital Resource CD (filename: equivalentnumbercards.pdf). At your signal, have students walk around the classroom and find other classmates whose cards have equivalent numbers.

2. Instruct students to sit together with their groups. Distribute an *Equivalent Numbers* activity sheet (page 148) to each group, and have the group members work together to explain the relationships between the numbers on their cards.

3. Review how to compare numbers and convert them from one form to another with the class.

4. Assign each group a fraction greater than 1 (e.g., $1\frac{3}{4}$). Have the group members work independently to convert the proper fraction into an improper fraction, a percentage, and a decimal using the *Converting Numbers* activity sheet (page 149).

5. Tell the group members to discuss how they converted the fractions into the other various forms. Give students time to compare their work and resolve any discrepancies.

Equivalent Numbers: One Quantity, Many Forms *(cont.)*

Apply/Analyze

6. Have students sit or stand in a circle. Explain how to play the *Reverse, Reverse!* strategy. (For detailed information on this strategy, see page 19.)

7. Choose a student to be the judge, and have him or her sit outside the circle. Instruct the judge to halt the game if, at any point, students say a number that does not follow the stated rule or relate to the number stated before.

8. Tell students that they need to say an equivalent number to the one said before in order to keep the game going in the same direction. Provide them with new starting numbers when they exhaust all options for a given number. Guide them through the first round of the game. Allow students to continue playing the game until the predetermined amount of time or number of rounds has passed.

Evaluate/Create

9. As a class, discuss the advantages, disadvantages, and practical applications of different forms of the same number (e.g., fractions for cooking, percentages for sale discounts).

10. Put the *Number Application Cards* in a bag or a bowl. Have each student pick a card.

11. Distribute the *My Word Problem* activity sheet (page 152) to students. Tell students to create word problems that involve changing the numbers on their *Number Application Card* to a different, more applicable form in order to solve the problems.

12. Assign each student a partner. Have students fold their *My Word Problem* activity sheets in half so only the problem is showing, and have them switch with their partners. On a separate sheet of paper, have students solve their partners' word problems. Give the pairs time to compare and discuss their answers.

Equivalent Number Cards

Teacher Directions: Cut apart the cards below. Distribute one to each student.

$\dfrac{5}{4}$	1.25	$1\frac{1}{4}$	125%
$\dfrac{2}{5}$	0.4	$\dfrac{4}{10}$	40%
$\dfrac{3}{8}$	0.375	$\dfrac{6}{16}$	37.5%
$\dfrac{8}{5}$	1.6	$1\frac{3}{5}$	160%

Equivalent Number Cards (cont.)

$\dfrac{9}{10}$	**0.9**	$\dfrac{27}{30}$	**90%**
$\dfrac{1}{2}$	**0.5**	$\dfrac{3}{6}$	**50%**
$\dfrac{3}{4}$	**0.75**	$\dfrac{6}{8}$	**75%**
$\dfrac{10}{4}$	**2.5**	$2\dfrac{1}{2}$	**250%**

Name: _____ Date: _____

Equivalent Numbers

Directions: Write the numbers from your group's cards in the appropriate boxes below. Explain the relationships among the numbers.

Fraction	Improper Fraction

Decimal	Percentage

Explanation

Name: _____   Date: _____

Converting Numbers

· ·

Directions: Write the fraction assigned to your group. Convert the fraction to the forms listed below, and show your work to explain how you reached each number.

Assigned Fraction	Improper Fraction

Decimal	Percentage

Explanation

Number Application Cards

Teacher Directions: Cut apart the cards below. Place them in a bag or a bowl. Allow each student to draw one card.

28%	$\dfrac{3}{4}$	**0.75**	$1\dfrac{1}{4}$
66%	$\dfrac{3}{5}$	**0.20**	$\dfrac{6}{3}$
80%	$\dfrac{9}{10}$	**1.2**	$\dfrac{9}{7}$
120%	$\dfrac{6}{7}$	**0.95**	$\dfrac{15}{3}$

Number Application Cards *(cont.)*

50%	$\dfrac{8}{9}$	**0.25**	$\dfrac{5}{2}$
150%	$\dfrac{2}{3}$	**0.55**	$\dfrac{10}{2}$
90%	$\dfrac{1}{3}$	**1.30**	$\dfrac{8}{6}$
10%	$\dfrac{2}{4}$	**0.70**	$1\dfrac{2}{3}$

 #51183—Brain-Powered Lessons to Engage All Learners

Name: _____ Date: _____

My Word Problem

....

Directions: Create a word problem that involves changing your chosen number into another more applicable form. Then, show how to solve your problem below the dotted line.

Chosen Number: _____

Word Problem: _____

_____

....

Word Problem Solution

_____

_____

_____

_____

_____

_____

_____

_____

_____

_____

_____

Inquiry and Investigation

Brain-Powered Strategy	Standard
Reverse, Reverse!	Designs and conducts a scientific investigation

Vocabulary Words

- data
- evidence
- hypothesis
- scientific method

Materials

- *Scientific Process* (pages 155–156)
- *My Experiment Design* (page 157)
- chart paper
- gummy candy
- glass of water
- experiment materials (*optional*)

Procedures

Model

1. Ask students, "What will happen when a gummy candy is placed in water?" Call on some students to share their predictions with the class and record their ideas on a sheet of chart paper.

2. Ask students how they could go about finding the answer to the question. Distribute the *Scientific Process* activity sheets (pages 155–156), and review the steps of the scientific method with the class. Have students follow along and complete their activity sheets.

3. Assign each student a partner, and give each pair a *My Experiment Design* activity sheet (page 157). Provide them with some basic background information on the composition of gummy candies. Have students work together to design experiments to test the predictions developed in Step 1.

4. Provide time for students to share their experiment designs with the class. Highlight the fact that there are many unknown variables that need to be accounted for in the experiment's design (e.g., How much water will be used? How long will the candy be in the water? What size/brand/type of candy?).

5. As a class, agree on an experiment design. Place a gummy candy in water, and make observations over the designated amount of time.

Inquiry and Investigation *(cont.)*

Apply/Analyze

6. Have students sit or stand in a circle. Explain how to play the *Reverse, Reverse!* strategy. (For detailed information on this strategy, see page 19.)

7. Choose a student to be the judge, and have him or her sit outside the circle. Instruct the judge to halt the game if students give a response that does not relate to the previous statement or that does not follow the order of the scientific method.

8. Give students a sample question (e.g., *How does water temperature affect the amount of sugar that will dissolve in the water?*). As they go around the circle, students need to give the steps of an experiment that could answer the question. Guide students through the first round of the game. Allow students to continue playing the game until the predetermined amount of time or number of rounds has passed.

Evaluate/Create

9. Working in small groups, partners, or independently, have students design their own experiment. Distribute new *My Experiment Design* activity sheets to record the steps. You may wish to provide sample questions for those students that need help getting started.

10. Have students switch their *My Experiment Design* activity sheets with another student or group. Provide time for students to revise their experiment designs based on the feedback they receive from their classmates.

11. If possible, allow students to conduct their experiments in class and test their hypotheses.

12. Display the student-designed experiments on posters or bulletin boards around the classroom.

Name: _____   Date: _____

Scientific Process

Directions: Read the statements listed below. Write them into the appropriate box to show the order of the scientific process.

COMMUNICATE RESULTS

READ PREVIOUS RESEARCH

RESULTS ALIGN WITH HYPOTHESIS

FORMULATE HYPOTHESIS

CONDUCT EXPERIMENT

ASK A QUESTION

RESULTS DO NOT ALIGN WITH HYPOTHESIS

ANALYZE DATA AND DRAW CONCLUSIONS

USE EXPERIMENTAL DATA AS BACKGROUND RESEARCH TO REFORMULATE HYPOTHESIS AND CONDUCT NEW EXPERIMENT

Name: _____ Date: _____

Scientific Process *(cont.)*

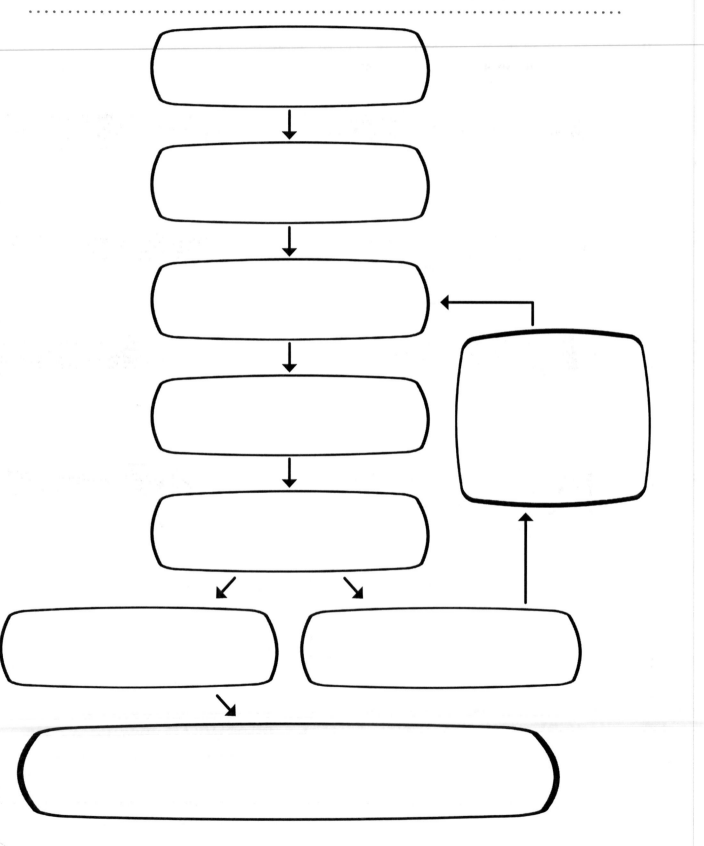

Name: _____ Date: _____

My Experiment Design

Directions: Record your question. Review previous research on the topic and formulate a hypothesis. Write down the materials required for the experiment and the necessary steps to test your hypothesis.

Question
Hypothesis
Materials
Experiment

List the Steps for Your Experiment

References Cited

Anderson, Lorin and David Krathwohl (Eds.). 2001. *Taxonomy for Learning, Teaching, and Assessing: A Revision of Bloom's Taxonomy of Educational Objectives.* Boston, MA: Pearson Education Group.

Baker, Linda. 2009. "Historical Roots of Inquiry in Metacognition." Retrieved from http://www.education.com/reference/article/metacognition.

Bloom, Benjamin (Ed.). 1956. *Taxonomy of Educational Objectives.* New York: David McKay Company.

Covington, Martin V. 2000. "Goal Theory, Motivation, and School Achievement: An Integrative Review." Retrieved from http://www2.csdm.qc.ca/SaintEmile/bernet/annexes/ASS6826/Covington2000.pdf.n.

Doidge, Norman. 2007. *The Brain That Changes Itself: Stories of Personal Triumph from the Frontiers of Brain Science.* New York, NY: Penguin Books.

Harris, Bryan, and Cassandra Goldberg. 2012. *75 Quick and Easy Solutions to Common Classroom Disruptions.* Florence, KY: Routledge.

Hunter, Madeline. 1993. *Enhancing Teaching.* Upper Saddle River, NJ: Prentice Hall.

Huntington's Outreach Program for Education, at Stanford (HOPES). 2010. "Neuroplasticity." http://www.stanford.edu/group/hopes/cgi-bin/wordpress/2010/06/neuroplasticity.

Jensen, Eric. 2005. *Teaching with the Brain in Mind.* Alexandria, VA: Association for Supervision and Curriculum Development.

Medina, J. 2008. *Brain Rules: 12 Principles for Surviving and Thriving at Work, Home, and School.* Seattle, WA: Pear Press.

Merzenich, Dr. Michael. 2013. *Soft-Wired: How the New Science of Brain Plasticity Can Change Your Life.* San Francisco, CA: Parnassus Publishing, LLC.

Overbaugh, Richard C. and Lynn Schultz. n.d. *Bloom's Taxonomy.* Retrieved from http://www.odu.edu/educ/roverbau/Bloom/blooms_taxonomy.htm.

Ratey, John J. 2008. *Spark: The Revolutionary New Science of Exercise and the Brain.* New York, NY: Little, Brown and Company.

Roth, LaVonna. 2012. *Brain-Powered Strategies to Engage All Learners.* Huntington Beach, CA: Shell Education.

Schenck, Jeb. 2005. "Teaching to the Brain." Retrieved from http://www.aa.edu/ftpimages/109/download/TeachingToTheBrain_Schenck.pdf.

References Cited *(cont.)*

Siegel, Daniel J. 2001. *The Developing Mind: Toward a Neurobiology of Interpersonal Experience.* New York: The Guilford Press.

Sousa, David A. 2006. *How the Brain Learns,* 3rd ed. Bloomington, IN: Solution Tree.

Sprenger, Marilee B. 1999. *Learning and Memory: The Brain in Action.* Alexandria, VA: Association for Supervision and Curriculum Development.

Thomas, Alice and Glenda Thorne. 2009. "How to Increase Higher Order Thinking." Retrieved from http://www.cdl.org/resourcelibrary/articles/HOT.php?type=subject&id=18.

Van Tassell, Gene. 2004 "Neural Pathway Development." Retrieved from http://www.brains.org/path.htm.

Vaynman, Shoshanna, Zhe Ying, and Fernando Gomez-Pinilla. "Hippocampal BDNF Mediates the Efficacy of Exercise on Synaptic Plasticity and Cognition." *European Journal of Neuroscience* 20 (2004): 2580–2590.

Webb, Norman L. "Alignment, Depth of Knowledge, and Change." Presented at the 50th annual meeting of the Florida Educational Research Association, Miami, FL. 2005. Abstract retrieved from http://facstaff.wcer.wisc.edu/normw/MIAMI%20FLORIDA%20 FINAL%20slides%2011-15-05.pdf.

Wiggins, Grant and Jay McTighe. *Understanding by Design (2nd ed.).* Upper Saddle River, NJ: Prentice Hall, 2005

Willis, Judy. 2006. *Research-Based Strategies to Ignite Student Learning.* Alexandria, VA: Association for Supervision and Curriculum Development (ASCD).

———. 2008. *How Your Child Learns Best: Brain-Friendly Strategies You Can Use to Ignite You Child's Learning and Increase School Success.* Naperville, IL: Sourcebooks, Inc.

'ofe, Pat and Ron Brandt. D. A. Sousa. 1998. *How the Brain Learns*, 3rd ed. Bloomington, N: Solution Tree.

Wyoming School Health and Physical Education. 2001. "Standards, Assessment, and Beyond." Retrieved May 25, 2006 from http://www.uwyo.edu/wyhpenet.

Contents of the Digital Resource CD

Pages	Lesson	Filename
29–33	M.A.I.N. Causes of World War I	causesofworldwarI.pdf
34–39	Express Yourself	expressyourself.pdf
40–45	Water and Weather	waterandweather.pdf
46–50	Thinking About Themes	thinkingaboutthemes.pdf
51–54	Themes Across Genres	themesacrossgenres.pdf
55–58; 54	Depression and Recession: Same or Different?	depressionrecession.pdf
59–61; 54	Perspectives on Anne Frank	annefrank.pdf
62–63	Roots of the Civil War	rootsofthecivilwar.pdf
64–66	Solar System Sculptures	solarsystemsculptures.pdf
67–68	Fascinating Figures (of Speech)	figuresofspeech.pdf
69–77	Precise Prose	preciseprose.pdf
78–82; 73–74	Variability in Pictures	variabilityinpictures.pdf
83–87; 73–74	Fascinating Fossils	fascinatingfossils.pdf
88–92	Making a Claim	makingaclaim.pdf
93–98	Lines and Planes: Mapping Rational Numbers	linesandplanes.pdf
99–104	Word Detective	worddetective.pdf
105–108	Revolutionary War Leaders	warleaders.pdf
109–115	Equivalent Expressions	expressions.pdf
116–120	Investigating Inferences	inferences.pdf
121–125	Perfect Paragraphs	perfectparagraphs.pdf
126–134; 124	Rad Ratios	radratios.pdf
135–139; 124	Energy: A Case of Multiple Identities	energy.pdf
140–143	Women and War	womenandwar.pdf
144–152	Equivalent Numbers: One Quantity, Many Forms	equivalentnumbers.pdf
153–157	Inquiry and Investigation	inquiryinvestigation.pdf

Pages	Additional Resource	Filename/ Folder Name
12–19	Strategy Overviews	strategyoverviews.pdf
25–28	Standards Chart	standards.pdf
NA	Enlarged Activity Cards (This folder contains the following PDFs: causescards.pdf, mathtermcards.pdf, watercyclecards.pdf, threelittlepigscards.pdf, bullycards.pdf, warleaderscards.pdf, mathexpressioncards.pdf, inferencecards.pdf, ratiocards.pdf, equivalentnumbercards.pdf)	Enlarged Cards
NA	Web Activity Sheets (This folder contains the following PDFs: causesweb.pdf, mathtermweb.pdf, watercyclewordweb.pdf, themewordweb.pdf.)	Web Activity Sheets
NA	No-Cook Dough Recipe	doughrecipe.pdf
NA	Depression Era Images	depressioneraimages.pdf